I0057973

Feet up by the Pool

How to Finance the Rest of Your Life
A DIY Guide to Saving and Investment

by
Jo Welman

Grosvenor House
Publishing Limited

All rights reserved
Copyright © Jo Welman, 2025

The right of Jo Welman to be identified as the author of this
work has been asserted in accordance with Section 78
of the Copyright, Designs and Patents Act 1988

The book cover is copyright to Jo Welman

This book is published by
Grosvenor House Publishing Ltd
Link House
140 The Broadway, Tolworth, Surrey, KT6 7HT.
www.grosvenorhousepublishing.co.uk

This book is sold subject to the conditions that it shall not, by way of
trade or otherwise, be lent, resold, hired out or otherwise circulated
without the author's or publisher's prior consent in any form of
binding or cover other than that in which it is published and
without a similar condition including this condition being
imposed on the subsequent purchaser.

A CIP record for this book
is available from the British Library

Paperback ISBN 978-1-80381-954-9
Hardback ISBN 978-1-80381-955-6
eBook ISBN 978-1-80381-956-3

The Author

Jo Welman had a career in the City spanning over 40 years and worked in a wide variety of financial and non-financial businesses. After graduating from Exeter University in 1979 with a degree in economics, Jo spent ten years at Baring Asset Management where he managed a range of UK and US pension funds and unit trusts, investing across multiple sectors including bonds, international equities, commercial and residential property and private equity.

In 1989 Jo was recruited to become Managing Director of merchant bank Rea Brothers' institutional and private wealth investment management division. Here he built on their sub scale funds management business and over the following decade launched a series of specialist investment trusts and funds in a variety of industry and property sectors, before forming a joint venture with reinsurance brokers Benfields (now Aon Benfield) and raising one of the first limited liability corporate capital vehicles for the Lloyds insurance market in 1993.

Following the sale of Rea to Close Brothers in 1999 Jo became Chairman of Brit Insurance Holdings Plc., a company that he had co-founded in 1995, and also served as non-executive director or chairman of several investment trusts and both publicly listed and private companies. In 2001 he founded a new private equity and specialist asset management firm, Epic Investment Partners (Epic). Epic was subsequently sold to AIM listed Syndicate Asset Management in 2010 but the private equity division remained independent and Jo was retained as an advisor to the management team.

Although now retired, Jo was invited onto the board as a Non-Exetuive Director of a Lloyd's managing agency and Non-Executive Chairman of a listed fund management group for his investment experience and continues to provide corporate finance and investment advice to entrepreneurs and private investors.

The Issues we now Face

The ways in which we live, travel and communicate have changed so very dramatically over my lifetime it is hardly surprising that we need to revisit and review many of our assumptions. I wrestle with Skype, Face time, Blogs, Twitter and interactive TV – all things that my children seem to understand as second nature.

This is nothing new – my grandfather was born in 1888, in an era of horse-drawn transport and warfare. He saw the first films, communicated on the first telephones, watched the first televisions, and even lived to see a man playing golf on the moon. But even though he was faced with equally dramatic technological and social change, I'm not at all sure that his basic financial assumptions were altered as fundamentally as ours in the 21st Century.

It is therefore hardly surprising that my generation needs help in understanding and coming to terms with the dramatic changes in the financial world in which we now live, and I hope this book can play some small part in helping some of my fellow baby-boomers and their sons and daughters to understand the ramifications. More particularly, I hope I can make readers aware of the potential dangers of handing down some of the outdated assumptions that served previous generations well, but may not hold true for our children.

None of the topics that I cover is unduly complex, but economics, finance and investment can be confusing to those unfamiliar with some of the issues and terminology. I hope that the book's guidance can give readers the confidence to take control of some or all of their investments, that they find the process interesting and fun and, most important of all, it allows them to retain more of the income that their investments generate.

On re-reading my first edition the book appears to cater for adults contemplating and saving for retirement, while my primary intention was to help younger people set out in life with at least some feel for the aspects of economics and the financial world that might influence their behaviour and life choices. As a result I have juggled the order of chapters and added some relevant topics so as not to bury those most relevant behind the more detailed investment thinking. I've also left Patsy's wonderful caricature of Gordon Brown on the book's cover. Brown as Chancellor was one of the main architects of the 'stealth taxes' that have undermined the benefits of saving for a pension.

If you are already into your forties or beyond I'm hoping that this advice doesn't come too late, but those of you leaving school or university and setting out on your working lives, please take on board the very boring necessity to take control of your financial future by starting a savings habit as soon as possible. I know life is tough with housing and living costs sky-rocketing, so I do understand that there's probably not going to be much left in the pot at the end of each month. And of *course* you'll want to meet mates in the pub and budget for holidays, but if you can find a way to start small and get into the habit of tucking a little away each month then at least it's a start.

When I embarked on the first edition of *Feet up be the Pool* in 2014 there were two motivating forces. The first that I refer to above, relates to the need for my children and their generation to start saving as soon as they start earning. The second was a genuine fear that those nearer retirement age could be in for a very nasty shock. In 2024 there does at last seem to be a growing awareness of the impending pension crisis, but the opportunity to warn people when to me it was becoming increasingly apparent ten years ago has been missed. We are approaching the time when a retiring generation faces the harsh realities of living off the income generated from a finite lump of savings. The shock of realising the extent to which many lifestyles will need to be dramatically cut back will prove distressing for many who haven't planned or saved sufficiently for life after they've stopped working.

The book's title 'Feet up by the Pool' is not intended as a smug 'look at me, I'm happily retired', quite the reverse – the book is an acknowledgment of the process I went through before retirement in my early 50's. Many like me want to stop work when we've had enough and not always when we've made enough! Whenever we decide to stop work we must understand our living costs and how much we need to have saved to fund them. I hope that this book might helps others through the same process.

"I hoped retirement would look like this."

All profits from sales of this book will be used to fund the provision of much needed financial education initiatives for secondary school and university students.

Contents

Introduction

A young man asked an old rich man how he made his money.

The old guy fingered his worsted wool vest and said:

*'Well, son, it was 1932. The depth of the Great Depression.
I was down to my last nickel. I invested that nickel in an apple.
I spent the entire day polishing the apple and, at the end
of the day, I sold the apple for ten cents.*

*The next morning, I invested those ten cents in two apples.
I spent the entire day polishing them and sold them at 5:00 pm
for 20 cents. I continued this system for a month,
by the end of which I'd accumulated a fortune of $1.37.*

Then my wife's father died and left us two million dollars.'

If my children are to accumulate enough capital over their working lives they are unlikely to achieve this by polishing apples – and they will only inherit if we die before we've spent the lot. So they need an understandable and contemporary overview of the financial options available to a generation that will, in the most part, rely on their own savings to provide for a comfortable existence when they eventually stop working.

For us Baby-Boomers who are already at or approaching retirement age, some of this advice might come too late, but we all need guidance through a very different financial world from the one that our parents inhabited. There is also a danger that the advice that we give our kids, inevitably a product of our own experience, is unlikely to be appropriate for this new world.

We must discourage our children from emulating our unhealthy focus on enrichment through borrowed money and home purchase. I always hoped that my children would one day own their own homes, but I did not encourage them to view this aspiration as an

"We want to put all our money into bricks."

investment to be traded, or as an alternative to saving. The risks and costs are now very considerable, and we should therefore encourage them to wait until they can see the prospect of job security and the likelihood that they will remain in the same location for some considerable time. This is why I do not believe that the value of their homes is likely to play such a significant role in their savings matrix – and why they must get into the savings habit as soon as possible.

In 2007 our children inherited a sum of money from their grandmother that allowed them a measure of independence during their university years. They were no better off in income terms than their peers who received similar and often larger allowances from their parents, but it forced them to make their own spending choices – they were off the parental payroll!

I manage their investments, and my objective has been to provide them with a combination of income and capital gain. I have also tried to convince them, successfully so far, of how much more difficult it is to accumulate capital than to spend it. As a result, they limited their spending to the income that their investments generate and when they needed more they found jobs.

Before I fall under the proverbial bus, I am determined to give them a sufficient understanding of finance and investment to avoid the many bear traps that they will encounter if they seek 'independent' advice – advice which, in my experience, is seldom truly independent, is often narrow in scope and sometimes worryingly ill informed.

So I wrote each of them a letter explaining a little of how the financial world works and how I am using the various investment tools at my disposal on their behalf. Given the size and complexities of the issues they will face over their working lives I believe these letters will prove woefully inadequate, so I decided to write this book for them to dust off when I'm not around, or for any fellow baby-boomers for whose children this advice might be relevant. Before embarking on this journey I first need to explain the tool of our trade.

Money

WILOT

"Oh, grandma, I know money doesn't grow on trees.
It comes outta that ATM machine at the mall."

Money is 'currency', a word derived from the Latin 'curren' - 'condition of flowing' - and is a term used for anything that is used as a medium of exchange. Before the introduction of monetary tokens such as coins and notes, barter was the common means of exchange. Barter is a system of trade where goods or services are directly traded without using money. I produce arrowheads for the hunter to kill deer and he pays me in the meat and skins that my arrows help him to shoot. You produce and sell corn and bread from your farm and I cook and clean your house in exchange. Your currency is therefore your hunting and farming skills and my currency is my skill in making arrow heads, cooking and cleaning.

When trades become removed from direct swap arrangements barter doesn't work. For instance I might wish to store the credits that I am owed from cooking and cleaning to spend sometime in the future – perhaps to buy fruit from another farmer. I therefore need some form of proof or accepted token or credit note to prove that I have credits in store for future purchases. I need money.

Our ancestors produced these tokens in the form of coins - often manufactured with rare and valuable metals which gave the holder confidence in its acceptance as a valuable currency. The predecessors of bank notes were notes issued by the Bank of England from the late 1600s. These were hand written 'promises to pay' and this promise was backed by a specific weight of gold. These promises became so popular the bank produced bank notes in fixed denominations rather than the random amounts requested by customers. A century later, to compensate for the lack of gold resulting from the French revolutionary wars at the end of the 18th Century, the Bank of England produced a £5 note, a one sided and fully printed 'white fiver' that remained in circulation until 1957.

The formal gold standard was first implemented by England, and the subsequent Bretton Woods system allowed $35 to be exchanged for an ounce of gold and maintained a system whereby currency continued to be backed by specified quantities of gold held in banks' vaults. This retained confidence that produce and labour were being exchanged for currency with real tangible value. After the first World War Britain had insufficient gold in its vaults to repay its war debts and the UK currency's 'Promise to Pay' was no longer backed by gold. In 1971 President Nixon finally terminated the convertibility of the US dollar into Gold and 'FIAT' currencies were born – currencies issued by governments without the backing of anything tangible. In Chapters 5 and 6 I describe what happens when the users of a currency lose faith and confidence in the value of this 'Promise to Pay'.

– THE NEW GOLD STANDARD –
2020

1

The Saving Habit

I SAVED ALL MY PENNIES IN A JAR AND DO YOU KNOW WHAT I HAD AFTER FIVE YEARS?

A JAR FULL OF PENNIES?

ROBERT THOMPSON

Get into the saving habit – and quick

Have you ever tried filling in an online personal pension forecast?
If not and you did, what might it conclude?

Simple Retirement Calculator: '*According to your latest figures, if you retired today, you could live very, very comfortably until 2 p.m. tomorrow.*'

Let's hope not, but after the peak in the household savings rate at about 20% of average earnings during the Covid lockdown (when we were unable to spend!) The average savings rate dropped back to around 8% and when wage increases fall below price rises this is likely to fall still further. This savings slump was the inevitable result of rising household expenses and falling real wages.

The Lucky Generation

For my parent's generation, UK employers assumed much of the responsibility for saving on their employee's behalf through the provision of guaranteed 'Defined Benefit' pensions. But, outside the public sector, pensions underwritten by employers and paid as a proportion of salaries prior to retirement have become increasingly rare. As a result most of us need to develop our own saving habit. My generation has treated home-ownership as a form of saving and a store of value which can be realised to help fund retirement through equity release loans or downsizing to a smaller home. With houses now so much less affordable, this option is less likely to work for our children, and so for them a savings habit is an urgent necessity.

I was born on the second day of 1958, so I'm a member of that lucky generation of post war 'Baby Boomers'. Wartime rationing had ended five years earlier, houses were still affordable, most people had Defined Benefit pensions guaranteed by their employers, and by the time we left school, personal tax rates had begun to fall from the dizzy heights they'd reached under the UK's socialist governments of the late 1960's and early 1970's. We *are* a lucky generation, and even though politicians of all persuasions have tucked into our pension savings through erosions in the tax benefits with great gusto, many of us own our homes, the value of which has multiplied over recent decades and can be extracted to fill any holes in our retirement arrangements. I fear that our children may not be so lucky.

But even my lucky generation faces some tricky issues. Despite the relative financial security that many of us enjoy as homeowners, we are the first generation for whom the majority will need to fund their lives after retirement from their own savings, rather than a guaranteed company pension. Worryingly, many are in danger of discovering this too late to put enough money aside to avoid a retirement in relative poverty.

The basic state pension is unlikely to cover much more that our utility bills, so it is vital that we gain an understanding of how we can plan and cope when we are no longer working. More importantly, our children need to be made aware of the issues they face as early in their adult lives as possible, because if they start the saving habit too late they will find it hard to catch up. Moreover they are likely to live for decades longer than their grandparents, and will therefore need to save and accumulate eye-watering sums if they are to fund a dignified and comfortable retirement over a much longer period.

Quite apart from the young who have sufficient time to plan, we all need to focus on the amounts we must save, how those sums should be invested, and the resulting income that our savings are likely to buy. So even if you are not young and you have not already planned your pension arrangements, this book's objective is to help ensure that you enjoy the longest, happiest, worry-free retirement possible.

2

Advisors Can No Longer Advise

FINANCIAL ADVISER

Cordell

"Shall I assume you're not overly risk-averse ?"

Our school curriculum appears to consider it to be more relevant and useful to learn about volcanoes and ancient history than some of the most essential life skills. As a result many of us lack the knowledge required to plan for life in an increasingly complex financial world.

Sources of Information and Advice

Our sources of financial information and advice range from ill-informed and questionably motivated politicians, many of whom have never held down a job outside politics and are therefore in no position to opine on any but the most basic financial issues, to 'Independent' Financial Advisors (IFA's). Many of the former seem to lack even the most basic understanding of todays' financial and economic issues, while the latter have, in large part, been forced into becoming product sales people, too constrained by their regulators to be able to offer constructive and individually tailored advice without fear of being sued or losing their regulatory licenses. Moreover their fees are such that only wealthier savers can afford to buy advice specific to their individual circumstances.

Then of course there are the banks on which many of us are forced to rely for financial advice. Don't get me started on them. The following story is just one example of the problem.

For the first time in over 40 years, my friend and gardener was contacted by his bank when they spotted a maturing endowment policy – and, of course, a potential fee for advice relating to the investment of the proceeds. Rapson (name changed) tends to seek my opinions on such matters, and I could only conclude that the advice offered by his reputable high street bank was both inappropriate and ill informed. I won't bore you with the detail, but it was obvious that the salesman's experience and competence was limited to a small number of products that his bank offers to smaller customers. This could have been fine if the range of solutions he was able to offer included something appropriate for Rapson's circumstances. Unfortunately, it did not.

Rapson subsequently received a visit from his pension adviser to discuss the investment of a maturing pension. He is in the bank's lowest risk client category, as defined by the regulator, meaning that his questionnaire suggested that Rapson's investments should be exposed to as little risk as possible. As a result, he suggested that Rapson uses his savings to buy a fixed income product that will pay him approximately £40 each month for the remainder of his life.

However, even if inflation falls and remains at or around 2.5% per annum, in ten years' time this £40 will be the equivalent to an income of under £32, and in twenty years, when Rapson is in his early eighties and perhaps need s to pay the extra cost of care, his annuity would provide under £25 per month measured in today's money. And this assumes that inflation does settle at 2.5%. If price inflation was to have remained at its recent double digit percentage levels – which before 2023 were last seen in the late 1970's, – then the £40 per month income figure could fall to the equivalent of under £5.50 within twenty years. When asked by Rapson if it would be better to accept a slightly lower immediate income and invest in assets whose income would grow, the IFA responded that the risk would be too high.

I would suggest that the advisor's proposed strategy carried the highest risk of all – the risk that Rapson's income from the investment would be insufficient to meet his needs. I will discuss these specific issues in greater detail in a later chapter, but my overall objective is to offer not only an understandable and contemporary overview of the financial options available to people like Rapson, but also to provide a template that is intended to give savers the confidence to make decisions about the allocation of, or even to manage, their own investments. To a generation that will, in the most part, rely on their own savings to provide for a comfortable existence when they eventually stop working, the former objective is a must, and success with the latter would be an added bonus.

This is not a technical manual, but the book's *minimum* objective is to arm readers with sufficient knowledge to allow them to ask more informed questions and to sense-check the financial advice that they receive, from whatever source. We also need to develop some basic life skills and disciplines. We need to budget our expenditure, understand about debt and, most important of all, understand why our homes should be viewed as places to live and not a substitute for saving.

3

'The Property Ladder' – There Are Snakes Too!

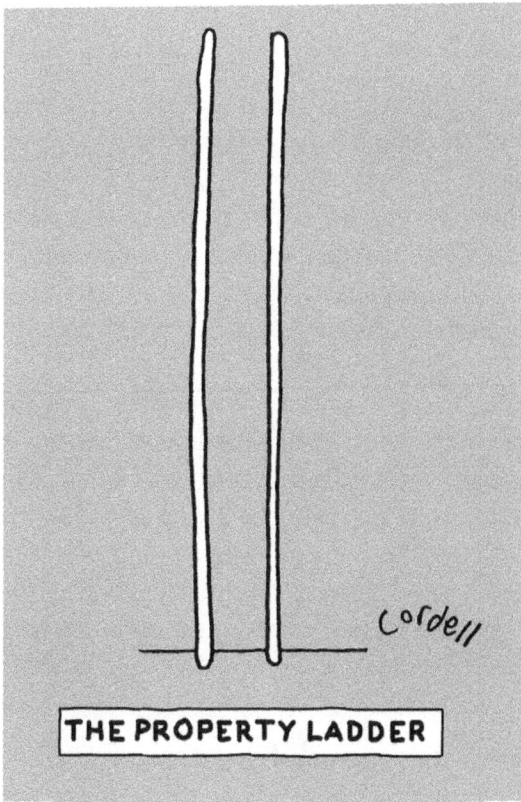

THE PROPERTY LADDER

In my introduction I contrasted the economic outlook for the post war home-owning Baby-Boomer generation with the likely prospects for our children. We should never underestimate our luck in having been able to afford to buy our own homes, the values of which might be available to enable us to fill any gaps in our pension and savings arrangements. However, if ever there was a prime example of my generation encouraging our children to do something inappropriate just because it worked for us, this could be it.

Let me explain what I believe has changed and why our advice might prove outdated and potentially dangerous.

'The Property Ladder'

Before sharing my concerns, let's start with a terminology issue. How often have we come across the stated determination to 'get onto the property ladder'? We've all played Snakes and Ladders and know what happens when our counter lands at the foot of a ladder – we go up. But when we arrive on the head of a snake? Herein lies the rub, because the use of this terminology exposes the dangerous assumption that property prices are a one way bet.

If the 'property ladder' worked for us, then why not for our children? Later in the book I will warn against relying on monetary assets to keep pace with price inflation and explain why long-term investors should invest in 'real' assets such as shares and property. To understand how the Baby-Boomers could afford to buy their homes we need first to understand the reasons why the Yield Gap between equities and Gilts reversed, and I will cover this in detail when I fully explain the case for investment in equities.

Inflation is the borrower's friend

I need to explain why it was such a cracking deal it was in the 1970's for the government to borrow, and then repay the loans a decade later after high inflation had eroded the real value of each £1 they had borrowed to nearer 35p. The government had, in effect, used inflation to decrease the value of its debts. Imagine now the benefits that *we*, ordinary people, also borrowed the money and repaid the bank ten years later after a period of high inflation.

Like the Government, we allowed inflation to erode the value of our debt, and so, like the government, we also repaid only a small proportion of the real value that we had originally borrowed. But *we* used the money we borrowed to buy a real asset that kept pace with inflation – our home. Using the same equation, this would mean that *we* borrowed a pound and repaid the equivalent value of say 35p after ten years, but the house that we bought for our loan of £1 was still worth in real, inflation-adjusted terms, the same as the £1 that we originally borrowed – three times the value of the debt.

Another way of explaining this phenomenon is to describe the actual mechanics of the trade. We borrowed the maximum allowed by banks and building societies in those days to buy our homes, which typically amounted to a multiple of between three and four times our annual salaries. A combination of high inflation and perhaps some job promotions pushed our salaries higher every year, and in turn we were encouraged to borrow three to four times this new, higher amount and buy a larger and more expensive property, and so on.

Over the next two decades, house prices rose with inflation and our salaries and the value of our homes soon dwarfed our debts, so we ended with little or no debt and owned houses that had multiplied many times in value. And the gains were tax free! Property had become a major source of wealth creation, but without help from high inflation many of us could not have built up the capital to buy the houses in which we now live.

So why can't our kids play this profitable game and use their homes as a core part of their savings matrix? Their biggest obstacle is affordability – particularly in the South East of England and the more affluent areas in and around London, where average house prices have risen so far as to be increasingly unaffordable to first time buyers. This has been caused by the combination of two factors – a massive imbalance of supply and demand, with too few new homes being built to cater for those seeking employment in the affluent South East – and record low interest rates which until 2023 had made large mortgages affordable. As a result, the three to four times borrowing multiple of average earnings today would neither buy a garage in central London nor a beach hut in Frinton-on-Sea.

Negative Equity

Irresponsible mortgage lending in the run up to the financial crash in 2008 made the problem much worse – many home buyers had borrowed too high a proportion of their home's value, so when prices fell, if they lost their jobs in the ensuing recession and were forced to sell their homes they could not achieve a price that allowed them to repay their lenders. The situation where the value of debt is greater than the value of a home is referred to as 'negative equity'. Let's hope we're not facing a repeat performance when the effects of higher mortgage rates filter through.

So how did our politicians try to ensure this did not happen again? For once, sense seemed to prevail and banks were discouraged from lending such a high proportion of a property's value. This in turn meant that first-time home buyers would be forced to save more for a deposit before they could buy a house and therefore owned a larger proportion of the value of their homes. As a result if they were ever forced to sell their homes they would be less likely to suffer from negative equity.

Very sensible you might think – and you would be right. But guess what? The Tories decided that their chances of re-election in 2015 were more important than either the fortunes of first time house buyers or the likely state of the British economy after the election. So they tried to buy votes by igniting another inflationary property boom, hoping that the 'feel-good factor' from rising house prices would spill over into improved consumer confidence, more high street spending – and more Tory votes. You don't need me to tell you how the previous credit fuelled consumer binge ended. Strong words, and so I need to explain how the blue touch-paper was lit under the housing market that lasted another seven years – and why.

IT'S A HANDY HOUSEHOLD DEVICE THAT HELPS CALCULATE YOUR NEGATIVE EQUITY

I must try not to get carried away with a political diatribe, but in 2015 I think it is fair to say that the rise of support for Nigel Farage and the UK Independence Party (UKIP) had meant that the Tories would require a series of unlikely miracles to deliver Mr. Cameron another term in a coalition government, let alone an overall majority of Tory MP's after the 2015 general election.

'One day, son, none of this will be yours...'

So with eighteen months to go, Mr. Cameron and his Chancellor came up with a ripping wheeze. The new 'responsible lending' criteria imposed on the banks after the 2008 Financial Crisis was, all of a sudden, no longer considered to be such a great idea after all. And so they decided to provide guarantees to enable young prospective Tory voters – oops, I mean the hard working, aspirational middle class families – to borrow up to 95% of the value of their new homes. Brilliant, let's replicate the conditions that bankrupted the Anglo Saxon world in 2008!

So the government – or rather you and I the tax payer – offered to guarantee the difference between what the banks would lend and the amount that house buyers actually need to borrow to secure their new home. It is hard to imagine a more foolhardy scheme, but it became obvious that home buyers would enjoy a wonderful party until the inevitable hangover that inevitably follows. Even the banks and building societies thought this was a bad idea – apart of course from the two banks that did agree to join the scheme. Lloyds and The Royal Bank of Scotland have one other thing in common – their largest shareholder was Her Majesty's Government who spent our money to rescue them from bankruptcy.

So there's no rush to get onto 'The Ladder'

Now I've got that off my chest, let's get back to the point. Whether or not I was proved right, record low interest rates have lured many house buyers into borrowing vast sums in relation to their current incomes, which has enabled them to clamber onto this so-called housing ladder. So what can possibly go wrong? As certainly as night follows day, it was obvious that interest rates would eventually rise again, and unless this was accompanied by a dramatic increase in wage inflation, it would cause many first time buyers to regret their high and potentially unaffordable levels of debt.

In 2023 this inevitable outcome came to pass – an explosion of inflation caused interest rates to rise very dramatically and the reasons why we have not seen greater falls in house prices are twofold. Many mortgages have their interest rates fixed and it is only when the fixed period expires that borrowers face increased interest costs. The second is that unemployment remains relatively low and it is when higher interest rates lead to losses of jobs that homeowners really do struggle to keep their homes.

And house prices from here? Even though valuations in London and the South East remain, by any historical criteria, ridiculously overstretched, there is no reason to believe that the supply/demand situation will deteriorate and cause a house price crash any time soon. That is unless or until the UK economy finds itself in recession that leads to job losses. But will we see another period of hyperinflation in house prices? No, not this time and not from these high and less affordable valuations, so our kids are unlikely to be able to inflate their way out of debt as quickly and easily as the post war baby-boomer generation. And there is one more secular change to consider.

Many of the current generations' careers will require them to be flexible and mobile as technological advances and changing global economic leadership make their working lives very much less static and predictable. Absent rampant house price inflation, the greatly increased costs of moving home imposed by successive governments through increases in stamp duty, means that the trading-up cycle that we enjoyed towards the end of the 20th century will no longer be a short cut to riches.

So we really mustn't encourage our children to emulate our unhealthy focus on enrichment through borrowed money and the purchase of residential property as part of their savings strategy. My children are fortunate enough to have bought homes during the recent period of low interest rates, but I have not encouraged them to view this aspiration as an investment to be traded or as an alternative to saving. The risks and costs are now very considerable, and therefore I believe that we should not encourage our children to borrow substantial sums to buy their home until they can see the prospect of job security (and with it the ability to pay higher interest on their mortgages) and the likelihood that they will remain in the same location for some considerable time.

This is why I do not believe that the value of their homes is likely to play such a significant role in this generation's savings matrix – and why they must get into a savings habit as early as possible.

4

Debt – When is it OK to Borrow?

"Begging or stealing are better options
than borrowing right now."

Before moving on to areas of investment, and without wishing to
embark on an exhaustive discussion of the uses and sources of
personal debt, I think it is important that we have an overall
understanding of the circumstances when we might need to
borrow, and some of the options and pitfalls. In particular, we
must differentiate between the types of spending for which we
borrow. In the context of retirement options and our discussions
of tax efficient investment strategies, the repayment of debt can
offer attractive returns.

When might we need to borrow?

Without wishing to patronise readers with mastery of the blindingly obvious, we borrow when we wish to purchase an item today and pay for it tomorrow, instead of saving up enough money beforehand. Most of us have needed to borrow to buy expensive capital items such as a house, motorcar or perhaps an expensive item of furniture. I would define debt-funded capital expenditure as spending on expensive items that we can use and enjoy for at least as long as it takes to repay a loan.

Loan periods for capital expenditure

When we buy our first home we typically take out a mortgage, secured on the value of the property and repayable over a period of twenty-five years or more. This is because the size of the typical loan required to buy a house will be a multiple of the buyer's annual income and so it will take many years to repay the lender out of our taxed income. Banks and building societies *allow* repayment of their loans over such long periods because a property's useful life typically exceeds the period of the loan and is therefore likely to retain or increase its value over that period.

The lender's loan is secured by a charge on the property for which the loan is required. In other words, if we cannot repay the loan or service the lender's interest, then the lender has the right to sell the property without our permission in order to have their loan repaid. The lender therefore needs to ensure that the property can be sold for a sum at least sufficient to repay their loan.

This is why banks and building societies insist we pay for an independent valuation and a survey of the property before they commit to a loan, just to ensure that there is nothing that could depress the value of the property or make it difficult to sell, such as rot, damp, ground subsidence, or any alterations that might have been done without the required planning permission and could be subject to dispute.

Now, compare a home purchase with a loan that we might need to buy a car. Although this too is a large item of capital expenditure, unlike our homes, most cars depreciate rapidly in value as they get older, so we should expect the loan to be made for a much shorter period so that it is repaid in full before the car becomes worthless, otherwise the lender will not have sufficient value to secure the repayment of the outstanding loan if the borrower defaults on the payments.

When we come to discuss investments we will relate investment to the matching of assets with our liabilities. The same principles apply with debt – the term of the loan should be less than the useful life of the asset that we are buying.

Current expenditure on credit

So why not use credit card funded borrowing or bank overdrafts to help cover day-to-day living expenses? We call this 'current' expenditure and we go back to the concept of matching loans to the useful life of the items that we purchase using debt. If we borrow to pay our rent, to pay for groceries or to fill the car up with petrol, then the useful life of these items is extremely short and unless the debt is immediately repaid, it will remain outstanding long after the item has been consumed or has any residual value.

In normal circumstances, we should avoid borrowing to finance current expenditure except for short term budgeting purposes – for instance to bridge a short gap before we are certain to receive the required funds, or to cover the occasional lumpy bill which we need to pay off over an extended period. We all have some chunky expenses and overheads that arise once or twice a year, such as club memberships, Christmas presents, car servicing, insurance or the winter quarters' electricity bills. These can often be spread through the year and paid by monthly direct instalments that remove the need for borrowing.

Reverting again to the need to match the timing of loan repayments to the useful life of the items purchased, if we borrow to fund current expenses we really must be certain of when the funds required to repay the debt will arrive, otherwise, as has happened to many families over recent years when incomes have failed to rise as fast as household bills, debts build up and rise beyond the borrower's ability to repay until there is no more credit available from their bank overdraft facilities, credit cards or even usurious payday loans, and they get into serious financial difficulties.

So what can we do if we can't afford to fill up the car or buy the groceries? I know it's easier said than done, but I refer to the budgeting disciplines that I will outline in a later chapter. If we can keep our overhead expenses such as rent, mortgage interest and utility bills below the level of our income, then we shouldn't need to borrow to fund current expenditure. If we can't, then more drastic action, such as a house move could be required to reduce the overheads.

Interest

When we borrow we are charged interest on our loan. I will cover interest payable on the government's borrowings in some detail in a later chapter when I cover investment in bonds, and some of the same principles apply to personal debt. The rate of interest we are charged by our lenders is a function of a number of factors, the first of which is the Bank of England's Base Rate. This is the interest rate that influences the rates at which banks and building societies both lend to us (and pay on our deposits) and as Base Rate rises and falls, our interest payments will usually move accordingly.

So we must make sure that we have not borrowed so much that a rise in the rate of interest could result in our inability to pay. In most circumstances we can fix the interest rate that we pay for a number of years so that this uncertainty is removed. This usually means that we will pay a higher rate of interest than would be charged on a variable interest rate loan, but we have the comfort of knowing that our interest payments will not increase for the period of the fix.

Repay Debt and Save Tax

It is often possible to increase returns and save tax by using our savings to repay debt, and here's an example of the arithmetic:

- We have a mortgage and other borrowings including credit cards totalling £150,000

- The average interest rate that we pay across all of these loans is 6% and our monthly payments therefore amount to £750

- We pay 40% higher rate income tax, and so we need to earn £1,250 each month just to pay the monthly interest

- Repaying debt is therefore the equivalent to a taxed investment return of £15,000 per annum from an investment of £150,000, so the debt repayment earns us the equivalent of 10% per annum

My final comment on the subject of interest rates and debt is that the market for loans is fiendishly complex and diverse, but here are some simple thoughts and guidelines that might prove useful:

- The proportion of the total value of what we buy that we need to fund through borrowing can affect the rate of interest that we pay on our loans. The lower the proportion we borrow, the more value and security the lender has to secure their repayment if we get into financial difficulties, and this will often affect the interest margin that they charge. The lower the lender's risk, the cheaper the loan

- Borrowing on a credit card is usually more expensive than arranging a bank overdraft – a short-term bank loan repayable on demand. If possible you should repay all of the outstanding amounts on your credit cards each month, and if there are times of the year when you need to borrow to fund additional expenses, then try to arrange an overdraft facility with your bank that allows you borrow small amounts from time to time

- The credit card market is highly competitive and many providers offer to wave interest for a period if you transfer your credit card debit balance to them and start using their card. However I cannot recommend this as a source of cheap borrowing because when you eventually start being charged interest the rates can be very high.

- Bank overdrafts are often unsecured and repayable without notice – which means that the bank does not have a specific asset as security that it can sell to retrieve its loan and so is usually more expensive than a loan that is secured against your assets.

- Bear in mind that banks sometimes charge a facility fee when they arrange or renew a loan or overdraft and this can greatly increase the overall cost of your loan.

- Beware introductory mortgage or credit card offers at very low interest rates and make sure that you can afford to pay the higher interest that will be charged when the interest rate reverts to its normal level.

- When we first take out a loan or have the use of a credit card, we start a credit history to which future lenders will have access, so when you apply for a mortgage, your credit history can be viewed by the prospective lender. Any blemish on your interest or loan repayment record, or even the failure to pay a utility or mobile phone bill, will affect your credit score, and in some cases can make it difficult to secure a mortgage. It can however be helpful to start using a credit card in order to build up a credit record because some lenders may not lend to people with no credit history.

If you are ever unfortunate enough to find yourself unable to pay the interest on your mortgage, don't be surprised if your account is moved away from the friendly people with whom you have communicated hitherto, to the 'recoveries' department. Here you will find people focused solely on recovering the bank's money by selling your home as quickly as possible and they have no interest in retaining any value for the borrower.

5

Money, a Trick of Confidence

"Of course it's fake money, you're
holding us up with a fake gun."

I left university in 1979 with a rugby player's second class honours degree in economics, but despite my degree I knew and understood very little about the way the UK economy really worked. So it is not without a certain irony that over 45 years later I am retired having lived through a variety of booms, busts, crises and recoveries and I believe that I now finally get it. If I was starting out as a fund manager today, I would be better prepared and infinitely more effective than that bright eyed and bushy tailed graduate who first reported for duty at Number 8, Bishopsgate in September 1979.

So before embarking on my attempt to simplify and explain the world of finance and investment, I need first to cover some very basic and fundamental economics, without which I can warn, with the benefit of my own experience, that it will be more difficult to understand the context in which we are investing our savings.

This is stuff we should all have been taught at school, and without wishing to sound overly arrogant or controversial, anyone entering a voting booth at an election who has no basic understanding of these issues might as well cast their vote blindfold.

The Economics of Free Market Capitalism

Before embarking on this potted economics tutorial perhaps I should first define the word 'economics'. The academic's definition is 'the study of the optimum use of scarce resources'. If there was an infinite supply of everything we need then it would not matter a jot whether we used resources efficiently. But there isn't. So economic theories have been developed to try and find the best methods of deciding how to allocate resources such as money, people, materials, industrial and office space, housing, healthcare – anything that is in limited supply. We're even now trying to allocate clean air – a resource that we had previously believed was infinite and therefore didn't need to be rationed or protected.

Modern capitalism was founded on free market economics – the assumption that, wherever possible, the market should be left alone to find the optimum allocation of resources. And how does 'the market' achieve this? Through two main levers – pricing and the profit motive. I believe that even Karl Marx acknowledged that the profit motive was an efficient mechanism for optimising the production process. The quantities and prices of goods produced and services provided are governed by the laws of supply and demand which, in the simplest of terms, adjusts prices up or down until the amount that people wish to buy is equal to the amount that others are prepared to produce and sell. Nobody does this specific calculation, but if the market is allowed to work efficiently and is left to its own devices, then this will be the logical outcome.

But of course the market isn't (and shouldn't always be) left to its own devices, and although there is no specific economic theory that promotes equality, we all know that if left to itself, some people will be left behind and wide differentials in living standards are inevitable. This is unacceptable and potentially dangerous outcome. So although measures that promote equality, such as progressive taxation, can dilute the efficient operation of the market mechanism, most people believe this is a price worth paying, and political disagreements now tend to revolve around the degree to which the free markets should either be managed and tempered or left to their own devices.

INFLATION IS WHEN EVERYONE IS SO RICH NOBODY CAN AFFORD ANYTHING.

Money and inflation – a trick of confidence

An understanding of what causes prices to rise, and the effects of inflation on our savings and investment returns is an important piece of the investment jigsaw. To understand inflation, we need to start from one of the most important underlying pillars of modern capitalism – confidence.

Have you ever considered why a supermarket will accept a £20 note or a contactless 'beep' in exchange for a basket of groceries? Why should a piece of paper with purple patterns and a picture of the King be so readily exchanged for £20 worth of goods?

The value of money

In 1822, Sterling as a currency became backed by gold, a commodity that for thousands of years has been accepted as a highly valued and trusted means of payment. The Romans used gold coinage, subsequently cutting regular grooves around each gold coin to stop people secretly shaving off some of the metal and debasing the currency. Thereafter, every £1 was backed by a specific weight of gold and it was the ability to convert currencies into gold that provided confidence in the underlying value of currencies that used this 'Gold Standard'.

The outbreak of the First World War left Britain with insufficient gold reserves to fund the war effort and so the gold backed value of Sterling was replaced by the British Government's 'promise to pay', a phrase that remains printed on Sterling banknotes to this day, alongside the signature of The Bank of England's Chief Cashier.

The lack of any tangible backing to the world's currencies has since become the norm – currencies are now termed 'FIAT' money, meaning that money is issued by the state and declared as legal tender by governments, but it is not convertible into anything tangible and therefore has no intrinsic value whatsoever. So why do we accept notes and coins with no intrinsic value in exchange for goods and services? Confidence – confidence in the governments' promises to pay, and, more pertinently, the confidence that those who accept payment in FIAT money can themselves use it to pay for other goods and services.

So what happens when confidence in the value of a country's money diminishes or evaporates altogether? I will cover various meltdown scenarios in a later chapter, but let's start with a well-documented example of Germany between the two world wars. The example itself leads neatly back to one of the primary causes of inflation.

After the First World War, as part of the surrender conditions, Germany was forced to agree to 'reparation' payments of compensation, primarily to France and Belgium. As these payments became increasingly unaffordable, the German government printed ever increasing billions of new Deutschemarks to buy American Dollars with which to pay the reparations. As a result the German currency's value was debased – billions of new Deutschemarks were in circulation chasing a limited supply of goods and services, and as a result prices started to rise. I'm sure you know how this story ended, but if not I will keep you in suspense until a later chapter. For the purposes of this discussion we can see why a debasing of the value of a currency' value – the amount it will buy – can lead to inflation.

What causes prices to rise?

Another way to describe inflation is that more money is required to buy the same amount of goods and services, and in the absence of any tangible backing for currencies it isn't hard to see why their values – the amount that a given unit of a currency will buy – might change over time.

There are two main underlying causes of inflation known as 'cost push' and 'demand pull'. Cost push inflation is caused by substantial increases in prices of input costs for goods where no suitable alternative is available. For example inflation rose sharply through the mid and late 1970's following a trebling in the price of crude oil. And again in 2021 when supplies were threatened by Russia's invasion of Ukraine. In the short term oil proved irreplaceable, and although alternatives were sought and consumption of oil fell, the economic consequences for non-oil producers in the 1970's were severe, and continued until the 'petrodollars' that had flowed out of these economies were recycled by the oil producing nations, helping to fund the economic growth that eventually kick-started a sharp recovery and economic prosperity though the following two decades.

The second equally common cause of inflation, 'demand pull', is when aggregate demand in the economy outpaces aggregate supply. In other words, there is too much money chasing too few goods and services, as happened in Germany between the wars.

Economic cycles tend to cause milder versions of this dynamic. After prolonged periods of growth, economies can face 'bottlenecks' and shortages in the supply of the resources required to fuel continued growth. After the period of Covid lockdowns and an almost total lack of economic activity, the supply chain was unable to quickly crank up supply and so the subsequent sharp recovery in demand caused prices to rise. These bottlenecks can take the form of shortages of materials and equipment, of skilled labour, or even of office and industrial work space, but shortages in the supply of any goods or services that cannot be readily substituted often leads to rising prices. The cures for this source of inflation are measures designed to cool demand until the supply of these resources can be increased sufficiently to eliminate the shortages, whereupon the economy can then return to some sort of balance, or 'equilibrium' – the point where demand can be satisfied by supply. At the time of writing the Bank of England and most developed nations's central banks have used the bluntest of tools – interest rates – to cool their economies and return inflation to their chosen targets.

The measures to which I refer can have significant effects on a number of variables that touch our lives and can also greatly influence the returns we might expect from our investments. It is therefore important that we gain an understanding of the tools at the disposal of governments to both minimise and manage the effects of economic cycles, whether these arise from wars, pandemics or any other causes of an imbalance between supply and demand. Economists are by no means of one mind in terms of the most effective of these tools and I will attempt to compress the Keynesian and Monetarist debate into a few short paragraphs.

Keynes vs. Monetarists

John Maynard Keynes was a British economist whose thinking caused a fundamental change in economic theory and founded a school of thought in the 1930's known as Keynesian Economics which was challenged by Monetarism, another school of economic thought, championed by the American economist and statistician Milton Friedman.

Monetarists believed that the main underlying cause of demand pull inflation was an oversupply of money in the system and that this oversupply must be removed if inflation becomes too high. To return to the example of Germany, too much money had been created and so there was more money chasing a finite supply of goods and services. There are two elements to money supply – the overall amount of money in circulation and the 'velocity of circulation'. Just because there might be too much money in the system, if it is hoarded and saved rather than spent then it will not necessarily lead to inflation.

Milton Friedman

John
Maynard
Kelynes
NAYLOR

For example, after the 2008 financial crisis Quantitative Easing ('QE') by central banks was a process that in effect created money in order to provide liquidity for the banks who were required to increase their reserves of capital so as not to be caught out again, but the reason this did not lead immediately to a significant increase in global inflation, was that the banks used this money to shore up their reserves against bad loans rather than pass it on to companies and individuals in the form of new loans. So in other words, although an additional supply of money had been created, it was not being spent or 'circulated'. Central bankers must have been hoping that when confidence returned and the money began to circulate, there would remain sufficient capacity in their economies to avoid the additional demand causing bottlenecks leading to higher inflation. I am of the strong opinion that the Bank of England continued with these expansionary monetary policies and low interest rates for at least a year beyond the obvious signs of inflation that became apparent towards the end of 2021. This failure accounted for much of the resulting over-tightening with much higher rates through 2023.

So how do monetarists advise governments to address this oversupply of money? Primarily through 'monetary base operations', which effectively regulate the supply of money in the system and interest rates which, when raised, deter borrowing and incentivise saving and therefore depress the demand in the economy for goods and services. High interest rates also increase the proportion of household incomes required to pay interest on loans and mortgages, and therefore decrease the amounts that households have at their disposal to spend, thereby further dampening demand.

Keynesians advocated more active fiscal policy to address the imbalances in an economy that can lead to both inflation and unemployment. By fiscal policy they mean the levels of government taxation and spending. Keynesians believed that even when the supply and demand of goods and services are balanced and in equilibrium, unemployment can remain too high, so the government needs to spend more to take up the slack in the economy, increase activity and provide employment. They believed that high inflation is best addressed through increasing taxes and decreasing government expenditure. The former removes individuals' spending power and slows demand, while the latter stops public spending 'crowding out' the private sector by releasing scarce resources that in turn helps to relieve inflationary bottlenecks.

Few economists would claim that the menu of measures described above represents an 'either, or' decision by the Treasury, it is more a question of emphasis.

Currencies and Exchange Rates

Early attempts at standardising currency.

Currency exchange rates can provide another tool or safety valve to cope with inflation. The exchange rates between currencies should in theory reflect 'purchasing power parity'. Surely when we convert pounds into another currency, the currency that we receive in exchange for our £1 should buy the same quantity of goods or services in that country? Well we all know from our overseas travels that this is seldom the case, but have you ever thought why?

The most obvious answer is that resource costs are not the same the world over – the cost of labour varies widely and taxes differ, as does the availability and cost of key resources. The latter point can sometimes be addressed by imports, but the costs of importing commodities such as cement and other bulky materials can be very considerable. So it is easy to understand why the cost of living varies widely from country to country. But this does not explain why currency exchange rates change, and here long term differences in inflation rates can play a significant role.

If prices are rising faster in one currency than another, then the currency exchange rate between the currencies provides a useful mechanism for adjusting their 'terms of trade'. By this I mean that trade between countries is partly a function of each county's 'competitive advantages'. Some countries provide some goods and services more efficiently and cheaply than others, and in theory we should be able to export our most competitively priced goods abroad and import other goods and services that are produced more cheaply and efficiently overseas. However, changes in relative currency exchange rates cause changes in the terms of trade. Goods priced in rising currencies become more expensive for importers with weaker currencies and vice versa. If currency moves merely cancel out their different inflation rates, then of course their terms of trade could remain unaltered. If not, the country with the weaker currency has a pricing advantage and will find it easier to sell its goods abroad.

I should add that since Russia's invasion of Ukraine and the Chinese threat to do likewise in Taiwan – and the competitive international scramble for Covid vaccines – competitive advantage is in many cases becoming a less compelling factor than the reliability of the supply of key products from domestic sources or 'friendly nations'. Perhaps the unseen result of the post Covid and post war shortages, is to spell the end of the world's headlong dash for increasing globalisation, and the sourcing of even the most strategically important supplies from any nation that can provide cheap alternatives through competitive advantages. For example it has become increasingly apparent that the UK must produce more of its own food rather than rely on imports.

After the 2008 financial crisis, the UK made use of the fact that it could allow its currency to fall relative to its trading partners and thereby improve the county's terms of trade, and therefore its ability to sell goods and services abroad. Currencies are not just a medium of exchange and a way of paying for goods, they are also used as a store of value, and the lowering of a country's interest rate relative to others can make it less attractive to hold and therefore can also form part of a strategy to cause the exchange rate to fall.

To investors with stronger currencies, despite Sterling's low interest rate, the UK suddenly looked a cheaper place to do business, or buy assets such as property, and this is one reason why the country's economy recovered more quickly than its European neighbours. Portugal, Greece, Ireland, Spain and Italy, the weaker members of the Eurozone, did not have this flexibility because they were locked into the Euro with their main trading partners. These countries to varying degrees found that without this ability to improve their competitiveness via weaker currencies, more painful debt and spending adjustments were forced onto them after the crisis. I will cover this in more detail in a later chapter.

The incoming President Donald Trump has indicated another method of addressing trade imbalances. A weaker Dollar would help America's terms of trade but as the world's reserve currency this isn't an option. Trump has indicated that he will resort to tariffs (taxes) on imports to make them less competitive and offer home producers the equivalent advantage that a weaker currency could offer.

6

Armageddon – When Money Doesn't Work

"MAY I HAVE MY ALLOWANCE IN GOLD BULLION?"

Although the chances of economic meltdown in a developed economy such as the UK are exceedingly small, history, and some of it quite recent, has shown that a complete breakdown of the assumptions behind free market capitalism can and does happen. The close interaction of both developed and developing economies means that the problems do not have to emanate from our own shores, or even our closest trading neighbours. Contagion can arrive from much further afield. So barring nuclear holocaust, what could cause such a breakdown? We come back to one of the foundations discussed earlier – confidence.

I have already covered Sterling's move from the Gold Standard to money issued on the back of the state's 'promise to pay', and it is this total lack of any tangible backing for FIAT money that can cause confidence in the value of money to evaporate. You may be surprised to hear how many currencies have become worthless over the past one hundred years and I have listed those countries and the dates of their currency meltdowns on the next page.

So let's return, as promised earlier, to the situation in the Weimar Republic of Germany between the world wars. I explained earlier that the printing of Deutschemarks to enable reparation payments to be made led to the hyperinflation that soon rendered the currency worthless.

Hyperinflation occurs when a country experiences very high and usually accelerating rates of monetary and price inflation causing the population to minimise their holdings of money, and under these conditions the official currency quickly loses real value. A medal commemorating Germany's hyperinflation in 1923 reads:

> *'On the 1st November 1923 one pound of bread cost three billion, one pound of meat thirty six billion and a glass of beer four billion Marks.'*

The German currency moved from one mark to one trillion marks to one gold-backed mark, and bank notes had lost so much value they were used as wallpaper.

So how did the French and Belgians get paid their reparations? Remember my reference in earlier chapters to the value of 'real' as opposed to monetary assets in times of inflation? Well here is a perfect example – the French occupied the Ruhr to ensure that the reparations continued to be paid in goods such as coal.

More recently Zimbabwe's hyperinflation began shortly after the destruction of the country's productive capacity in their civil war, and the subsequent confiscation of private farms. During the peak month of inflation in November 2008, inflation reached over six trillion per cent rendering the currency completely worthless. In 2009 Zimbabwe abandoned its currency, which in 2014 still had not been replaced and they used other countries' currencies to trade.

Other currency collapses have taken place in countries with foreign debt crises when they can neither service (pay interest) or repay their debt – Argentina's Peso suffered twelve thousand per cent inflation in 1989. France's during their revolution was of course a lot earlier. Other countries that have suffered hyperinflation include:

- Angola 1991-1995
- Argentina 1989
- Armenia 1992-1994
- Austria 1914-1923
- Azerbaijan 1991-1994
- Belarus 1994-2002
- Bolivia 1984-1986
- Brazil 1967-1994
- Bulgaria 1997
- Chile 1973
- China 1948-1949
- Estonia 1992
- France 1795-1796
- Georgia 1992 and 1994
- Germany 1923
- Hungary 1923-1924
- Kazakstan 1992-1993
- Kyrigystan 1992
- Serbia 1992-1993
- North Korea 2009-2011
- Nicaragua 1986-1990
- Peru 1988-1990
- Philippines 1942-1944
- Poland 1923-1924 and 1989-1990
- Russia/Soviet Union 1921-1922 and 1992
- Taiwan 1945-1948
- Tajakistan 1992-1995
- Ukraine 1992-1996
- Uzbekistan 1992
- Yugoslavia 1992
- Zaire 1993-1998
- Zimbabwe 2008-2009

Quite a list. Many of these coincided with wars or revolutions, some, as I mentioned earlier, related to indebtedness and the country's insolvency, and it is on the latter theme that I return to the global financial crisis of 2008 which spread contagion throughout both developed and developing economies, and some uncomfortably close to home.

Before we get too smug about other countries' currency meltdowns, bear in mind that currencies such as the US dollar and UK Pound have also depreciated to almost zero - it's just taken very much longer! £100 in 1964 was worth £6.60 by the beginning of 2024*. So in just 50 years the Pound has lost over 90% of its value.Even if UK inflation remains at only 2% per annum, £1 will be worth only 13p in 100 year's time, and at 5% (not an unreasonable possibility given the recent history) £1 shrinks to 1p in 82 years!

Do Crypto Currencies such as Bitcoin Provide an Answer?

"This is Pete, our cryptocurrency expert."

A cryptocurrency is a digital or virtual currency secured by cryptographic systems which allow secure online payments.

---

*CPI Inflation Calculator

Most use blockchain technology – a set of connected blocks of information on an online ledger. Each block contains an independently verified set of transactions. The fact that this network is distributed across a large number of decentralised computers allows it to exist outside the control of governments and central authorities. The advantages include cheaper and faster money transfers, but as a store of value their prices have been very volatile. Imagine if the value of your £20 note could rise or fall dramatically on a day to day basis and you have little idea how much you will need to do the weekend shop!

One major advantage to criminals is that payments can be made away from the scrutiny of tax authorities and the police. Another unwelcome attribute is the huge amounts of energy required to create or administer cryptocurrencies. Central Banks and regulators are busy trying to bring these new currencies into their sphere of monitoring and regulation and fear the wider consequences their increasing use – and the knock-on effects if their huge valuations collapse.

Cryptocurrency was originally designed as new currency with a fixed and finite supply, free of central bank interference and the inflationary printing of more and more currency. This might just have worked if these currencies had remained as tokens of exchange and hadn't become 'stores of value', traded aggressively by private and institutional investors. American hedge funds are now major players, and having built up huge holdings of crypto find a growing range of ways to tempt new investors to enter at higher and higher prices in order not to miss out. The arrival of President Trump in the White House, a vocal supporter of Cryptocurrency has added fuel to this fire.

The concept of a short cut to extreme wealth is promoted by celebrities who in many cases have endorsed these currencies and derivatives of them in the world of digital art. Like any such trade, it relies on the greater fool theory – a worthless asset being passed on to another greedy investor hoping to get rich quick. Crypto has become a Ponzi Scheme, very much along the lines of Berni Madoff who defrauded wealthy investors in New York out of $65 billion. He was imprisoned but Crypto has remained 'legit'. I suppose you can't blame these currencies, just the people who manipulate them, but when the music on this merry go round stops, get rid quick – remember the golden chain letters in the 1990s? In the meantime I'm sure their values will be talked up higher and higher.

My personal view is that cryptocurrencies are here to stay but values will remain volatile and there will be circumstance when – as with national currencies over the past two hundred years – their values could collapse to zero. And remember that unlike national currencies, there are no governments or central banks to step in to support them. I believe that any investment in cryptocurrencies has no basis of value is therefore akin to a trip to the bookies at a race track. Even successful FIAT currencies such as the American Dollar have no intrinsic value, but are much less likely to depreciate significantly between leaving home and arriving at the supermarket! However even sceptics such as me have to concede that as a store of value over the longer term, the values of cryptocurrencies are no more unpredictable than even the major national currencies whose supply remains at the whim of a central bank's printing press.

Banks

We return to the theme of confidence, but this time it is confidence in the country's banking system. Banks provide the mechanism through which money is transmitted and flows through an economy, and confidence in the bank's collective strength and solvency has become as important as confidence in the underlying currency.

Like FIAT money, banks are a trick of confidence. We deposit money with them on the assumption that our money is safe. The banks are forced by their regulators to keep sufficient funds available to provide liquidity for their depositor's needs, while the remainder is loaned out to people and companies for varying periods.

But what would happen if every depositor, even with one of the world's largest and strongest banks, turned up on the same day to withdraw their money? Well of course the money just isn't there and it could take many years for the bank to retrieve all of its loans, some of which – such as residential mortgages – are contracted for considerable periods, and so in theory the bank would be insolvent. It is only the confidence that our money is safe that allows banks to operate and to lend a large proportion of our deposits to their customers. So what could cause our confidence in the banks to be sufficiently shaken to cause a run on their deposits?

Remember the BBC television coverage of Northern Rock Building Society's depositors queuing up to withdraw their funds in 2008? Why do you think this happened?

Banks regularly lend each other their spare money overnight through the 'interbank market', and some smaller banks and building societies with smaller customer deposit bases who make long term loans to house buyers, traditionally relied on this interbank market for a proportion of their funding. Suddenly, after the demise of Lehman Brothers, banks lost confidence in the safety of other banks – particularly small banks and building societies. As a result word got out that these banks were short of funding and, not helped by soothing comments from The Chancellor that drew attention to the issue, panic set in with depositors who scrabbled to remove their funds, making the situation even worse. So confidence can evaporate very quickly, even in well-known and reputable household names on our own doorstep.

It was not until, after days of prevarication and more soothing comments from the then Chancellor Alistair Darling, that the Bank of England finally announced that in order to end the panic and restore confidence it would provide sufficient liquidity and guarantees to depositors. To prevent two much larger banks going the same way as Northern Rock, the Government was forced to go a stage further and spend eye-watering sums of taxpayer's money to buy shares in Lloyds and RBS which subsequently merged with NatWest. This demonstrated the importance of confidence, and once confidence has evaporated, decisive and aggressive measures can be required to restore confidence in the entire financial system – banks, money, everything. Do remember

THAT MONEY WE WITHDREW FROM OUR ACCOUNT – THE BANK WANTS TO BORROW IT BACK

that such measures would not be mobilised on behalf of digital currencies operating outside the financial system.

Governments and central banks have now learned from previous episodes that when confidence evaporates the first thing that they must provide is sufficient liquidity for the banks to convince the public that their money is safe. In 2008 the Bank of England started creating money and pumping liquidity into the UK banking system, but, unlike Germany's money printing spree in the 1920's, they delivered some tough talk about controlling the UK's inflation and debt, otherwise the pound could have suffered a similar fate to the Deutschmark – interest rates would have risen to attract investors to defend the value of Sterling assets, confidence would have been further damaged and the problem could have escalated further.

Deflation fears

AAACHOOO! AAACHOOO! AAACHOOO! AAACHOOO! AAACHOOO!

GREECE   ITALY   SPAIN   IRELAND   PORTUGAL

GERMANY

-PLETCH-

CONTAGIOUS WARD, EURO-ZONE DEBT CRISIS

In 2008 the fear was not of inflation but *de*flation. It was the fear that if the population was to lose their collective confidence in their economic future and stop spending altogether, then the prices of goods and assets could actually fall, and the last thing that over-indebted banks and households could afford was to see a collapse in the value of their assets – particularly the residential properties on which so many loans are secured.

The banks' bad loans – loans that were in danger of going into default and not being repaid – were a serious enough problem without the value of the assets securing these loans collapsing in value. The subsequent increase in the supply of money through Quantitative Easing (QE), which entailed the Bank of England creating money to buy the most risky assets from the banks, succeeded in averting deflation and together with an interest rate of next to nothing, QE created a subsequent asset price boom in both stock markets and property that helped avert the threat of a financial meltdown.

The central bank's job in such situations is to restore confidence by convincing their populations and their overseas creditors, investors and trading partners that their money and their banks are safe. The UK government even increased the size and range of their deposit protection scheme – a government guarantee that depositors who lost money if their bank went insolvent would be fully compensated – up to a maximum of £85,000 at the time of writing. Such was the fear of a downward spiral in confidence, the Treasury was prepared to do almost anything to restore confidence in the banking system – even to the extent of guaranteeing deposits and buying large shareholdings in Lloyds and RBS.

From a UK domestic investor's standpoint, after the initial wobble the years following the crisis were a bonanza. Low interest rates forced investors to search for higher returns from bonds, equities and property and as a result values recovered very smartly. However this binge continued far too long and values rose too far. The economy's sharp rebound from the Covid lockdowns in 2021 met supply constraints which prevented the supply of goods meeting this sudden surge in demand. Inflation was on the rise long before Russia's invasion of Ukraine and the resulting squeeze on energy and food supplies. The Bank of England continued with almost zero interest rates for at least a year beyond these clear inflation signals and this in turn caused very dramatic increases in interest rates in an attempt to return inflation to their 2% target.

Some were not as lucky as the UK

—KANDALAFT—

"I am pleased to present
Greece's new currency—
the Gyro Sandwich."

In 2008 other weaker and even more indebted Eurozone countries such as Greece and Portugal were not so lucky. Although they were locked into the Euro, meaning that at least there could be no question of their domestic currencies suffering a hyper-inflationary meltdown, being locked into a strong currency meant they could *not* bring their interest rates down and allow a weaker currency to take some of the strain from their collapsing economies.

In the inflation section I referred to the advantage gained by the UK from depreciating the pound and thereby both attracting buyers for Sterling denominated assets such as London property, and making it easier for British companies to export their cheaper goods and services to overseas customers. This option wasn't available to the weaker members of the Eurozone who were forced to go cap in hand to Germany for the loans they needed in order to stave off bankruptcy. There was a point when Greece was unable to pay public workers without a bailout and would most certainly have been added to the above list of currency meltdowns if the country had retained the Drachma.

So we can conclude that among the developed nations, because of fears that the meltdown in one currency can endanger the economies of its financial and trading partners, the stronger economies are likely to provide the rescue loans required to avert a collapse in confidence that could lead to hyperinflation and a disintegration of a currency's value.

So far it has been smaller economies that have needed assistance and so these loans have been affordable – just – but one wouldn't bet the house on Europe's collective ability to do the same for one of the larger members of the Eurozone such as Italy or even France. For Greece the medicine that has been enforced on their economy in exchange for the bail outs proved very divisive. Massive cutbacks in public spending made life very tough, even for those in work, and the resulting danger of civil unrest was very real indeed.

But if the worst does happen....

So what if the worst does happen and a country goes bust, it cannot be rescued, and its money becomes worthless? Countries can and have come back from such events and rebuilt confidence in a reconstructed economy and a new currency, but an event that could cause country of the size of the UK to fail in isolation, though hard to contemplate, would be truly seismic.

It would show mastery of the blindingly obvious to conclude that monetary assets, ineffective insurance against inflation in normal times, would not be the place to shelter funds if inflation accelerates and the value of money is undermined. But if we are in a 'Mad Max' scenario of social meltdown and anarchy, the values of our equity and property investments might not provide much comfort either.

Gold

As persecuted German and Polish Jews in the 1930's and early 1940's would confirm, assets that are not transportable can be of little value when populations are displaced. So we come all the way back to gold. Gold has remained a store of value over thousands of years, and in times of greatest fear and uncertainty, the commodity's universal acceptance and its ability to facilitate the transport of large amounts of wealth will increase both its popularity and value. I will always hold gold – physical bars and coins – as an insurance policy, while hoping that insurance is never required!

So just for fun let's end with a league table of assets that might be high on the popularity list come the revolution when all rights to property disappear and armed militias roam the streets:

Useful Stuff

- Gold and precious stones
- Weapons and ammunition
- Tins of food

- Lighters and matches
- Warm clothing and strong boots
- A tent
- A cave
- 4WD Car and 100 cans of fuel

Useless Stuff

- Cash
- Gilts
- Shares
- Hedge Funds
- Houses
- Branded leather goods
- Monogrammed slippers

This might seem a rather facetious analysis, but not to German Jews in the 1920's and 1930's, not to white Zimbabwean farmers in 2008, not to the Romanov Royal family in 1918, Serbian Muslims in 1992 Syrian, Burmese or Afghan or Palestinian refugees today.

"Does it say what we use for money?"

7

Brexit – Why did the
UK Vote to Leave?

This seems appropriate time to discuss Brexit – the vote taken
in 2016 for the UK to leave the European Union, supported
by 51.89% of those who chose to vote – arguably too fine a
margin for this momentous decision and outcome. Having made
reference to the aftermath to the 2008 Financial Crisis and the
outcomes for individual members of the Eurozone (different to
the EU, just those countries that exchanged their individual
domestic currencies for the Euro), a discussion of Brexit seems
appropriate.

A Bit of History

The European Coal and Steel Community (ECSC) was created after the second world war to integrate core industries into a single common market. It was formally established in 1951 by the Treaty of Paris and signed by Belgium, France, Italy, Luxemberg, the Netherlands and West Germany. The ECSC's subsequent enlargement in both the number of members and the organisation's duties ultimately led to the creation of the European Union. Britain applied to join in 1963 and again in 1967 but on both occasions the application was vetoed by General De Gaulle, the President of France, because he judged Britain not to agree with the core concept of integration. How right he was!

However the green light for UK's membership was finally given in 1969 and talks began the following year. The UK finally joined The European Economic Community on 1st January 1973. De Gaulle was ultimately proved right – the UK saw what subsequently became the EU to be a trading partner rather than a firm commitment for ever closer political and economic union. Perhaps it was the small strip of water between the UK and Continental Europe that had proved so successful in protecting these islands since the 11th Century that removed the political will to use EU membership as a means to fully integrate with Continental Europe.

Much of Europe remained understandably scarred with insecurity having had their borders threatened in two world wars. It was under the leadership of Margaret Thatcher that the UK's relationship with the EU came under particular strain. The signing of the Maastricht Treaty in February 1992 announcing conversion criteria for a new era of greater European integration that brought the UK's commitment to ever closer union with Europe to a head.

The Treaty was signed by John Major who as prime minister was determined to present a less confrontational attitude towards the EU than Mrs Thatcher. However the UK's signature was conditional on the removal of the word 'Federal', an opt out from the Social Chapter which covered areas such as employment rights and health & safety, Britain was not to be committed to monetary union (replacement of the Pound by the Euro) and managed to devolve more decisions away from the EU towards national governments. Many British eurosceptics felt this was a 'treaty too far' and this led to divisions within the Tory party between factions with greater and lesser appetites for closer integration with other EU countries.

In December 2011 Prime Minister David Cameron plunged the UK's position in Europe into further uncertainty after he used his veto to block a treaty imposing greater financial regulation on EU members and a new Euro regime. From that moment there was a two speed Europe with Britain excluded from meetings concerning the Euro and financial regulation and Cameron warned that the UK's continued membership of the EU could not be guaranteed. He was himself not in the eurosceptic camp, but was forced to concede due to a significant and powerful eurosceptic faction within his party. His ambition was for the EU to accept a two speed Europe with Britain outside the Euro. Many in the UK believed that they were voting for an economic union in which Britain traded freely with Europe without trade barriers or tariffs, but never accepted the prospect of a political union where Europe governed increasing areas of day to day life – even to the extent that a UK market trader continuing to use Imperial measurements – pounds and ounces rather than kilos – was committing a criminal offence.

A proposal for a referendum on the UK's continued membership was intended as a threat to persuade the EU to accept the UK's opt outs and less subservient relationship. Cameron's specific requests did not appear dramatic or overly controversial, but perhaps because the EU did not believe that a public vote for the UK to leave the EU could possibly succeed, David Cameron returned almost empty handed. As an EU enthusiast, Cameron put the most positive spin possible on the small concessions that he achieved, but we now know that the die was cast. Even so, it was the popular and charismatic Boris Johnson's decision to lead the 'Leave' campaign which tipped the balance in favour of a narrow defeat of the 'Remainers' in 2016. The subsequent demise of Johnson's political career has lent credence to the Remainer's view that we were persuaded to vote ourselves out of Europe on the back of dodgy statistics and outright lies. The reality was less simple.

It has subsequently transpired that there was a wide variety of reasons why so many people voted to leave the EU and there is a popular view expounded by bitter Remainers that younger Britons and Euro enthusiastic Scots were dragged out of the EU by lies and English working class anti-immigration racists. There is no question that working class voters who perceived that free movement within the EU was inundating their towns with Eastern Europeans overwhelming public services and the jobs market. Although I was a committed Leaver I believe that the availability of pools of European labour was one of the greatest advantages of the UK's EU membership. Following the pandemic it is apparent that, post Brexit, the shortage of labour has proved very damaging to many sectors of the UK economy and in particular pubs and restaurants that continued for some years to struggle in this regard.

Many disagree vehemently, but I believe that despite short term disruption and the Tory Government's lack of post Brexit vision and poorly negotiated post Brexit trading arrangements, there were compelling reasons to believe that the UK's longer term economic outlook could be greatly enhanced by independence from European rule. The EU is presented as an organisation that promotes free trade, but it is in fact a highly protectionist clique, determined to limit competition with non-European economies and to trade tariff-free just among themselves. It is becoming increasingly apparent that both the UK and EU remain in an over-regulated and over taxed economic slow lane and are being shown a clean pair of heals by the Far East nations and the United States. You only need travel to America to see how little a Pound or a Euro will now buy, while twenty years ago a visit to New York was a bargain hunt for European travellers. However it is my belief that the most damaging and dangerous longer term issue relates to the Euro.

Since the Brexit vote, ardent 'Remainers' have used every statistic available to persuade those that voted to leave the EU to 'Bregret'. There has been plenty of ammunition to fire at the Brexit outcome and the UK's triumph in leading the way on Covid vaccinations away from the EU's bureaucracy and in-fighting has now been forgotten, as the UK's anaemic economic performance and stubbornly high inflation have been conveniently laid at the door of Brexit. As a 'Leaver' I readily concede that any benefits from Brexit were swamped both by the Covid lockdown's disruption to economic activity and a hapless Tory Government's total absence of planning or vision. I believe Boris Johnson was as surprised at the outcome of the referendum as any.

The result has provided scant evidence of benefits from the UK's new-found freedoms to form its own laws, regulations and trading arrangements, and the post Brexit era has got off to a decidedly shaky start. However the Government was forced to focus on mightier economic storms that arrived at our shores from the Covid pandemic and subsequent wars in Ukraine and the Middle East, and it remains hard to differentiate and expose the culprits for the economy's subsequent lacklustre performance. One can only concede that the added complications and frictions resulting from our extrication from Europe after half a century of membership cannot have helped.

Any 'Bregrets'?

However before we throw in the towel we need only to look at the subsequent performance of the German economy, by some margin the largest in the EU, to put the UK's post Brexit woes into a less damning context. Over recent years the IMF (International Monetary Fund) has appeared determined to paint the UK as the sick man of Europe, while at the time of writing, scrutiny of the numbers suggests that the UK economy continues to outperform Germany and France on many measurements and would be comfortably mid-table if the UK had remained in the EU – despite the frictions from leaving the European free trade block. Remember the UK was running a huge trade deficit with the EU, meaning that imports far outweighed the value of goods and services sold into Europe. As a result it is understandable that the UK's trade balance with Europe since Brexit has outperformed expectations.

We will only know with the benefit of a much longer period of hind-sight to judge whether the UK's decision to leave was an act of self harm or a longer term economic necessity. However I would bet a pound to a penny that if successfully harvested, the benefits of othe UK's detachment from a highly bureaucratic and unarguably corrupt system of European government – which embraces the worst 'race to the bottom' aspects of collective socialism – will serve future generations well. As a country we should be looking both east and west towards growing regions of the global economy that embrace democracy and free market economic policies.

Europe will continue to protect itself from outside competition to trade merrily among themselves. Outside the EU, the UK can do better, much *much* better, but to do so we must rely on our politicians to up their game – tax less and leave businesses freer to trade without overly burdensome EU regulations.

Is the Euro a Disaster Waiting to Happen?

Either by accident or design, the European common currency has served to enrich Germans and impoverish its smaller and weaker southern European members. The concept of a single currency and a common monetary policy that's appropriate at any one time for each and every one of the 23 members of the Eurozone was never a realistic outcome. Before the creation of the Euro, the

'Deutschmark Block', (Germany, Austria, Holland, Luxembourg, Belgium and France) had effectively converged to a sufficient extent that made the progression to a common currency both feasible and logical. Having returned from a holiday which entailed a stay on the Germany/France border, it now seems inconceivable that the two countries can share such a huge and unmanned border and still operate different currencies. However the initial list also included Finland, Ireland, Italy, Portugal and Spain where the Euro entry criteria were fudged to allow membership of countries whose economies operated with very different dynamics.

The obvious advantages of a common currency for trade between these countries were that imports and exports would not be subject to changes in their relative exchange rates and neither would there be the additional uncertainty and 'frictional' cost of buying and selling each other's currencies, so on the face of it, a common currency was a sensible idea. The initial eleven participants in the Euro in 1998 were keen that other EU members followed suit when their convergence criteria were met and Greece, Malta, Slovakia, Slovenia, Estonia and Cyprus now make up the full compliment of 23 with Denmark and the UK obliged to join when their economies met the convergence criteria.

It soon became obvious that initial concerns about the membership of these weaker economies proved well founded. Many (including me, guided by my mentor in such matters, Sir Alan Walters) could clearly see that the acceptance of countries that had very obviously *not* met the convergence criteria for entry into the Euro was a recipe for disaster – as is typical when a political agenda trumps economic reality.

Things chugged along OK for several years until the new currency met its first real test during the financial crisis in 2008. The necessity for 23 disparate economies to manage the economic cycle and a recession with one common currency (and interest rate), proved a recipe for trouble. How can Germany, a huge economy that manufactures machinery and quality motor cars expect to be synchronised with Greece, Portugal, Italy, Ireland and Spain? The answer is that it could not. Moreover the Eurozone's strict fiscal rules relating to the proportion of each country's Gross Domestic Product that could be borrowed to cover government expenditure and to provide economic support, has not been evenly applied, with enormous French deficits, way in excess of the set criteria, remaining unpunished.

Weaker Eurozone members were not as lucky as the UK

In 2008, weaker and even more indebted countries such as Greece and Portugal were not as lucky as the UK which had remained outside the Euro. Although they were locked into the Euro and there could be no question of their domestic currencies suffering a hyper-inflationary meltdown, being trapped in a strong currency meant they could not bring down their interest rates and the value of their currencies to allow cheaper funding and a weaker currency to help them compete and take some of the strain from their collapsing economies, as their products, services (and tourism) would become cheaper for overseas customers.

The UK took full advantage of an independent currency by allowing the pound to depreciate and thereby both attracting buyers for assets valued in Sterling such as London property, and making it easier for British companies to compete and export goods and services to foreign customers. This option wasn't available to the weaker members of the Eurozone who were forced to go cap in hand the EU for the loans they needed in order to stave off bankruptcy. There even came a point when Greece was unable to pay public sector workers without a bailout and, had they retained the Drachma, would most certainly have been added to my list of currency meltdowns. The actual outcome was almost as bad, with plummeting real incomes and soaring unemployment.

So we can conclude that among developed nations, because of fears that the meltdown in one currency can endanger the economies of its trading partners, stronger economies continue to provide the loans and support required to avert a collapse in confidence and further contagion. So far it has been smaller economies that have needed assistance and so this support has been just about affordable, but one wouldn't bet the house on Europe's collective ability to do the same for one of the larger members of the Eurozone such as Italy or even France. For Greece the medicine that was enforced on their economy in exchange for bail outs was particularly tough, even for those in work, with massive cutbacks in public spending and a very real danger of civil unrest.

The Euro has enriched Germans and impoverished the weaker members of the Eurozone

Much is made of China's huge trade surpluses with the rest of the world – and subsidies which have allowed the country's exports to threaten local industries such as steel manufacture. However Germany's much larger surplus seemed to have slipped below the radar. Germany's advantages did not mirror China's obvious anti-competitive subsidies and cheap labour – theirs was the ability that the Euro offers to keep the German exchange rate locked with their weaker European trading partners. Outside the Euro, German trade surpluses would have driven the Deutschemark higher and made the rest of Europe's goods and services relatively cheaper and more competitive. The Euro has therefore over a long period served to enrich Germany and impoverished much of the Eurozone.

In order for countries such as Greece to improve their competitive position, they needed to do one of two things. They could allow their currency (formerly the Drachma) to fall relative to their trading partners – a policy no longer available due to the country's Eurozone membership – or improve their economy's competitiveness relative to their trading partner countries through increased productivity, meaning an increase in the amount the country produces relative to the amount of resources that are used. It was never realistic for Greece to outstrip Germany's productivity gains through increased technology investment and efficiencies over the extended period required for the Greek economy to catch up and eradicate the trade deficits. And so Greece's only recourse under a regime imposed on the country by the EU was to further impoverish Greeks through draconian government spending cuts in exchange for loans, leading to an explosion in unemployment and appalling falls in disposable household incomes and living standards. Happily there are now signs that Greece has made significant progress – although at the expense of a 15 year period of falling living standards. Ironically it is an ailing motor industry and expensive energy costs that followed the embargo on Russian gas imports that pushed *Germany* into the economic infirmary.

How could the common currency be made to work?

So how could the obvious failings of the single currency be addressed without impoverishing large numbers of the populations of its weaker and less productive members? When local economies with a common currency in the regions of the UK suffer relative to London and the Southeast of England, regional discrepancies in household incomes and employment prospects are addressed through the reallocation of tax revenues to investment and subsidies in the weaker regions. This is referred to as Regional Policy. Taxpayers in the more successful regions where core employment is related to growing services (such as the financial services sector in London) seem to accept this reallocation as an obvious requirement within their country – now quaintly termed as 'levelling up' by our politicians looking for a useful election marketing slogan.

Such a reallocation of resources within the EU requires a similar attitude towards the redistribution of resources between member countries which is not quite such an easy sell. The underlying problem with the common currency will not be solved by a similar regional redistribution policy between countries over the long term – which in times of economic stress and hardship risks popular protests and a lurch to populist right wing governments. No, if the Euro is to succeed and survive its members must agree to a true USE – a United State of Europe with one central bank, common laws and taxes. You cannot just have a common interest rate and allow individual states to retain control of the other tools of economic management, and under a USE regime no EU member can retain its own currency and remain outside the Eurozone. I believe that European leaders already realise this but cannot see a way to convince voters to accept such wholesale sacrifices of national economic management and sovereignty. Such a move might strengthen recent moves to right wing, anti-Europe populist member state governments. The current fudge will therefore continue and will only serve to hold back the entire trading block. Not a promising outlook.

8

Investment Risk

"I sleep poorly anyway, so you might
as well put me in high-risk investments."

Once we have bought into the savings habit, our investment strategies for the money that we save must be structured in the context of what we need our savings to achieve. In order to achieve an above inflation return, these savings must be exposed to an element of risk, so we must first define and explain investment risk.

Cash is always the lowest risk investment – right? Wrong.

Let's analyse and define risk. Not all the fancy hedge fund malarkey, just risk as we all understand it. Here are the three categories of risk that I believe are most relevant to us – the risk of loss, liquidity risk and investment risk.

Risk of Loss

Without wishing again to display a mastery of the blindingly obvious, I define this risk as the possibility that an investment could be valued or needs to be sold at a lower price than you originally paid for it.

Sales at losses don't always result in a negative return if an investment has generated more income than the capital loss, but that aside, investors suffer loss if investments are sold after their value has fallen, but the *decision* to sell at a loss can often be justified and should not always be feared. Investments should be sold below their purchase prices either when there is a better investment opportunity for the funds elsewhere, or perhaps because some unforeseen circumstance requires the raising of cash at an inopportune moment, depriving us of the opportunity to wait for the value of an investment to recover. Or we just make a mistake, circumstances change and we don't believe the investment's value will recover. It happens.

My definition sounds rather pedantic, but even though we must accept that we might occasionally lose money in an investment, it is vital to ensure that our original purchase decision was appropriate in the context of what the invested money was intended to achieve at that time. More on that later, but let's try and grade investments according to the risk of loss.

Unless the bank where you deposit your money goes bust*, cash deposits must rank at the bottom end of the risk of loss matrix, followed by government bonds, followed by high grade company bonds – debt issued by companies that offer a higher rate of income than Gilts issued by the government – then shares and property, then unquoted equity and venture capital. This list is not intended to be exhaustive, but it covers the main asset categories at the disposal of most private investors. I will cover these categories later in more detail.

The industry term that best describes risk of loss is 'volatility' – the extent to which the realisable values rise or fall on a day to day basis. The daily ups and downs in the individual share prices of companies that make up a stock exchange do not necessarily reflect constantly changing views of the prospects for each company. It is much simpler than that. In the short term, the price of any share is purely a function of supply and demand, so if more investors wish to sell than buy, the price will fall and if there are more buyers than sellers then the price is likely to rise. Simple. Investors' day-to-day reasons for buying and selling can be many and varied and may not always relate directly to the outlook for each individual underlying company. However over much longer periods truth will out, and the performance of the underlying investment over an extended period *should* be reflected in the valuation of their shares.

The moral of the story? Don't buy volatile assets for short investment periods. Buying shares for short-term gain *is* gambling, but a long-term commitment to shares is not. This is why I get so irritated when financial commentators refer to stock market investment as a gamble. I heard the lady who ran SAGA using the word several times in a short interview on Breakfast TV and felt like throwing something at the screen!

---

*Banks that are covered by the Bank of England's Depositor Protection Scheme currently have up to £85,000 of every depositor's funds guaranteed

Most of us, whether we realise it or not, are exposed in some way to equity markets, and quite rightly so. To refer to equity investment as a gamble is both incorrect and irresponsible. More on this later, but I would recommend a study by Ibbotson Associates, an American research business entitled *The Reduction of Risk Over Time* which related risk to different holding periods between 1926 and 2011. Ibbotson's study confirmed our assumption that overall volatility and the risk of loss decreases over time, meaning the longer the holding period, the less the risk of loss from equity investment.

What Ibbotson's research showed was that volatility falls over longer holding periods, and although there have been many individual years, and even some longer periods, when equity investments in America have shown substantial negative returns, despite the *huge* falls over the Great Depression and stock market crash of the 1930's and another very severe bear market in the early 1970's, markets have always recovered and there has *never* been a twenty year investment period when owners of US shares have suffered negative returns.

Liquidity Risk

Whether or not an investment has been historically volatile, some assets are easier, quicker and cheaper to sell than others. This is sometimes referred to as 'liquidity risk'.

Although share prices of large company shares can be volatile, it is at least possible to buy and sell large quantities cheaply and quickly. There is therefore very little liquidity risk. Conversely when we deposit cash with a bank for a fixed period of time in order to take advantage of a better interest rate on offer, there is often a cost if we suddenly find ourselves in need of the cash due to some unforeseen circumstance. There may be no volatility risk but there *is* some liquidity risk. Property is often viewed as being less volatile than shares, but properties can be particularly difficult and expensive to sell in a hurry. So there is no guarantee that an investor will receive full value if the proceeds from the sale of a property are required urgently.

Liquidity is an important issue for insurance companies exposed to unexpected events such as major natural disasters, because the timing of big insurance claims is not something that insurance companies can either forecast or control, so they hold a large proportion of their funds in liquid assets. Like them, we often need to sacrifice the high returns that can be available from less liquid assets because we too are likely to be faced with an unexpected need for cash – maybe an urgent roof repair, a speeding fine or even a surprise tax demand. You get the picture.

Investment Risk

This is the risk that really matters to the long-term saver. This risk can best be described as the risk that our investments fail to meet our objectives. In this context I now return to my previous statement that cash cannot always be considered to be a low risk investment.

Financial advisers are forced by their regulators to assess every client's 'risk appetite', and this risk is often related exclusively to the risk of loss. But this narrow perspective misses the point and is merely a form of arse-covering. The financial regulator's focus on the suitability of the investment advice that we receive is more often than not confused with our capacity to cope with losses, and fear of short term falls in the value of investments can prevent advisors from offering appropriate guidance to their clients.

However the regulators also insist that financial advisers abide by the 'Know Your Client' (KYC) directive and this in turn *should* allow for a more holistic approach that would enable IFA's to offer advice that directly relates to our individual circumstances. Let me explain.

The phrase that I and others use to describe this process is the 'matching of assets to liabilities', but in layman's English the objective is to ensure that our mix of assets is, and remains, the most likely to achieve our objectives – defined as the eventual purpose for which the money will be needed. But there is one important aspect missing from this description, and that relates to risk.

If any investment advisor believes that their task amounts to anything more than the achievement of their clients' objectives with as little exposure to risk as they can get away with, then they've totally missed the point. That *has* to be their objective, plain and simple.

So before we start, we need to know:

- What the money is needed for
- When it is needed ?
- What could change that might require a review of our plans?

It is only when we understand the intended use of the money that we can structure an appropriate mix of assets to achieve these objectives. We now need to focus on the requirement to match our assets to our liabilities. So what type of investment provides the best and lowest risk match for your stated objectives? This decision can be best explained by three simple illustrations of some differing objectives, each requiring different strategies. Note that the *timing* of these requirements is the major determinant of investment strategy:

- **Liability**   **Tax demand in six weeks' time**
- Matching Asset   *Cash*
- Why   *We need liquidity and certainty of value in six weeks.*
- Risk   *None*

- **Liability**   **School fees to be paid in 3 years**
- Matching Asset   *Fixed dated 3 year bond or bank deposit*

- Why   *The return of capital is guaranteed in 3 years*

- Risk   *None. There's no investment or liquidity risk because the bond matures before the fees become payable*

- **Liability**   **A pension income in 35 years' time**
- Matching Assets   *Shares, property, private equity etc. ('real' assets)*
- Why   *Best match for real, long-term liabilities*
- Risk   *Only investment risk is relevant – volatility and illiquidity don't matter over longer holding periods*

So what *is* our risk?

Let's now go back to our long-term savings and pensions. As I've suggested in the third example above, if the money is to remain invested for several decades then the *only* relevant risk out of those described above is investment risk – the risk that the investments we select do not achieve our objectives. Do we care about day-to-day volatility? No we don't. Neither do we mind losing the ability to sell quickly, because the assets can remain invested for long enough for their lack of immediate liquidity not to impose a constraint on our investment selections, and in some markets such as bonds, investors are typically rewarded with higher interest rates if the bonds are either long dated or unlisted and are more volatile or cannot be easily sold.

So if we define a matching asset as the best match for a known liability, should we not invest *all* of our money in the best matching asset? I will cover the ways in which we can mitigate risk in a later chapter, but there are many reasons not to place every egg in the same basket, particularly when we are accepting a level of risk in order to achieve real long-term returns.

No investment can be 100% risk-free, but some are less risky and their returns more predictable than others. For instance it is unusual, but governments have gone bust, banks have needed rescuing from bankruptcy and even the largest 'blue chip' companies can perform badly for extended periods and have very occasionally even gone bust. So no investment is totally without risk – even cash hidden under the mattress can be stolen or lost in a house fire!

Diversification

We can mitigate risk by diversifying our assets, and we can diversify both between asset types and between investments within the same asset category. For instance, even large cash deposits can be spread between different banks to take advantage of the government's deposit protection scheme that guarantees up to a maximum sum per depositor if the bank gets into difficulties. I will cover the allocation of our assets in more detail later, but it is important to understand that over 90% of investment performance has historically been generated by the *type* of assets we invest in, rather than our ability to select the best individual investments within each of the asset categories.

9

The Death of Pensions.
What Now?

FINANCIAL
ADVICE

CHAFF.

*"It's never too late to improve
the deficit in your retirement savings - ever
considered a life of crime?"*

Despite the much lauded changes in George Osborne's 2014 Spring Budget, the improved flexibility that his measures introduced do not address the fundamental issues and particularly for those approaching retirement. Yes, the measures provide incentives to save more via ISA's and pensions but they do not address the immediate problems that relate to older employees who's pension funds and other savings are likely to prove inadequate. Moreover they do not equip pensioners with all the products, advice and knowledge required to use this additional flexibility safely.

Pensions – problems and some solutions

"I challenge your assertion that your solution to the pensions crisis is 'highly original', Perkins... it appears to be merely the plot of the film 'Logan's Run'."

Many who are approaching retirement are confronted with some tough choices, particularly those who discover late in their working lives that their savings are unlikely to prove sufficient to provide them with an acceptable living standard for their increasing lifespans. These choices could involve us resorting to the equity value that many own in their homes, either through down-sizing to a smaller house or some form of 'equity release' – mechanisms that allow home owners to remain in their homes while releasing some of this value in a loan to meet living costs not adequately covered by their pensions or other savings.

However we try to assemble the savings required to fund our retirement, those (now the majority) of us who do not have a Defined Benefits (DB) pension arrangement need to understand the risk to which these savings will need to be exposed if we are to generate sufficient income for our needs.

My parent's generation (and those of you lucky enough still to belong to such schemes – mostly public sector employees) were typically members of DB schemes which, as the title suggests, offered an income post retirement that was clearly defined and related to the number of years they had worked and been part of a scheme, and how much they earned in their final working years. These schemes are also known as 'Final Salary Schemes' because of this relationship. Retirees could therefore forecast with a high degree of certainty the amount of income that they would receive for the remainder of their lives and could plan their retirements accordingly.

The Death of Pensions

For a number of reasons, companies that guaranteed their employees' retirement incomes concluded that this liability had become too costly.

In many cases, following periods of relatively low interest rates and low investment returns, the investments that had been set aside to provide employee pensions were in danger of proving insufficient to meet these costs and so pension deficits forced companies to increase pension fund contributions out of their profits.

But the main factor behind the decision to end DB schemes in the private sector was their employees' increasing life expectancies, and with longer lives come longer retirements during which pensioners would expect to continue drawing pensions. As life expectancies increased, the provision of pensions became so expensive that the risk to the employers who were guaranteeing them was unacceptable.

As a direct result, the majority of us, either as part of a company funded scheme where our employers make contributions to our pensions, or as a personal pension plan such as a SIPP (Self Invested Pension Plan) where we do it all ourselves, put aside a proportion of our salaries to be invested in order to build up a fund of savings from which to provide income for our retirement. These are referred to as Defined Contribution (DC) schemes. The difference is that if these savings prove insufficient to fund a decent pension, there is no company to make up the difference – the risk of a shortfall is now born by us.

Before moving on to possible options and strategies to cope with this new responsibility, here is another rant. I've already taken mild swipes at politicians and banks, but nothing to compare to this. Before proceeding I would point out that the culprits over recent decades do not inhabit one political party, but Gordon Brown's underhand and mean spirited tax raid on our pensions did take the biscuit – and was another major contributor to the pension's disaster that looms. The subsequent coalition and Tory governments have exacerbated his subterfuge; so don't start me on that lot either!

Many readers will be unaware of the gold plated pensions that we tax payers fund for our self-serving politicians. Suffice to say that after a relatively short political career Mr. Brown receives a guaranteed pension, indexed for inflation for the remainder of his life. Lucky Gordon, Lucky David, Theresa, Boris, Liz and Rishi (and Sir Kier!). It is therefore particularly galling that former Chancellors have changed the ACT rules (don't worry about the detail– it means that they now tax the previously untaxed dividends earned by our pension funds' investments) which, when combined with the other factors that have increased the cost and risk to companies, provided the final nail in the DB scheme coffin and have contributed directly to the impending pensions crisis. Because of the extended period over which the effect of the tax compounds and becomes visible, this 'stealth tax' was a quite clever way of raising more tax without being immediately spotted by the victims, but the long-term effects are devastating.

Administrations of all colours have since followed Mr. Brown's lead, and seeing pensions as a soft touch, they have progressively chipped away at these important tax-efficient savings arrangements. This they have achieved by decreasing the sums that we can set aside tax free in any one individual year.

All of these measures increase the Treasury's tax revenues in the short term, but have stored up an unaffordable problems which will be brutally exposed long after those responsible have left the scene of their crimes. Admittedly these latter raids will mainly affect higher rate taxpayers – their effects are again focused on a section of the population they refer to as their favoured 'hard working' middle classes whose votes they crave, more and more of whom have been sucked into higher rate tax brackets by non-indexed, static personal income tax bands. This is the section of the population that I fear is in for the biggest shock of all when they approach retirement and realise their pension arrangements are woefully inadequate and will not provide enough income to maintain their pre-retirement living standards.

Apart from getting this tirade off my chest, it is important that we understand the longer-term effects of these stealth taxes. As I say, due to the length of the political cycle, the results of these raids on our future capacity to fund a dignified retirement are only felt long after the perpetrators have left the crime scene and are enjoying their own well-funded retirements – paid for in part by these additional taxes on *our* pensions. So what can we do – work longer, retire later?

These are the inevitable outcomes, and one for which I cannot lay the entire blame on our politicians. Previously, pension arrangements were designed to provide retirement incomes for an average life expectancy of around 78 years. Retirement at the age of 63 would therefore be predicated on an average of 15 years over which income from our company pensions would be required. The same arrangements cannot be expected to cater adequately for an increased life expectancy and the resulting extension of the period when we will need to draw our pensions.

Simple arithmetic shows that a 5% increase in life expectancy from 78 to 82 years increases the funding requirement from 15 to 19 years – an increase of over 25%. As life expectancies increase the position deteriorates, and so it would be unrealistic (unless of course you are French) to expect to maintain the same retirement age. The government has already acknowledged this outlook by increasing the age at which we receive our state pensions. I dread to think what our kids' ages will be before they begin to receive their state pensions – the number will probably begin with at a seven.

**"You can afford to retire at 65, but
you'll need to die at 70."**

My vision is of the mythological Tantalus, who stood in a pool of water beneath a fruit tree and when he reached up for the fruit it moved out of reach, and when he bent down for a drink the pool receded. I fear that our children may get close to, but never quite reach, the state's chosen (and regularly increasing) retirement age. So these grapes may never be picked and I will also bet a pound to a penny that one day the basic state pension will become means tested along with many other 'universal benefits' for which we pay over our working lives.

So we must save more?

Certainly – and not exclusively via pensions, but more on that later. As important as the proportion of our income we set aside for retirement is the period over which we save. The earlier we can start the better, and for many who have delayed it may be difficult to catch up.

When our kids are setting up home and worrying about mortgages, household bills and holidays, it's hard for them to focus on the need to start saving. With mine I have resorted to some simple arithmetic – the power of compounding. I hope that readers will not feel patronised by the analysis below, but it does deliver an important message. Compounding is the ability of an asset to generate earnings, which are then reinvested in order to generate their own earnings. In other words, compounding refers to generating earnings from previous earnings

Let's make a couple of basic assumptions and compare the outcomes for two young people, one who starts saving at the age of 23, and another who waits another seven years until the age of 30:

Saver A

- Saves £100 per month
- **Starts saving aged 23**

- Retires aged 66
- Annual investment return 5%
- Lump sum at retirement £364,000*

Saver B

- Saves £100 per month
- **Starts saving aged 30**
- Retires aged 66
- Annual investment return 5%
- Lump sum at retirement £245,000*

So it really is quite simple, a seven-year head start using identical assumptions increases the total sum saved by nearly 50% and this is due to the power of compounding returns. This is by no means an extreme example – many do not believe they can or need to start saving until much later in life, but as we can see, by then it becomes even more difficult. You don't need to be Albert Einstein to spot that every year's delay adds a year onto the other end of our working lives, and by the time our kids arrive at the current retirement age it will be much worse, because the majority could be expecting to survive into their second century.

Change investment and saving strategies and assumptions?

Yes, yes and yes again. Saving more and for longer is a given, it's a truism, its mastery of the blindingly obvious, but in understanding the investment options most of us need help, because these are relatively complex issues that require careful explanation, even to some of those who believe themselves to be financially literate.

Annual Compounding

So this is why over the early chapters I have risked boring the more financially aware by starting at the most basic level of understanding, before I attempt to convince readers that our financial assumptions and behaviour will need to change if we are to avoid fearing the time in our lives when we stop working.

After a lifetime of work we really shouldn't dread the period of our lives that can be the most enjoyable. I've now retired and believe me, life doesn't get any better than this, so let's agree how we can plan for the time that we stop work.

10

Budgeting for Retirement

'You're right... It is our state pension.'

However diligent we are in saving for our retirement, few are able accumulate enough capital to be confident of maintaining their pre-retirement lifestyles without some disciplined budgeting and prioritisation of expenditure. Even DB schemes work on a ratio of two thirds of retirees leaving salary. This planning exercise should take place before we retire, and is a discipline that perhaps we should all have begun long before we were even contemplating retirement, because unless we understand our expenditure patterns before we stop earning, we could be in for a nasty shock when we do.

Household expenditure should be viewed as a pyramid. The base of the pyramid represents basic, necessary expenses that we all incur to keep a roof over our heads and to eat, and the layers of the pyramid rise towards the pinnacle of discretionary, non-essential expenditure on the luxuries and treats that we might hope still to afford when we stop work.

So try breaking your current expenditure down into sub categories:

Fixed Overheads

These are items of expenditure that are fixed and must be paid every month of each year. They include:

- Rent or mortgage interest
- Council Tax
- Water Rates
- Electricity
- Gas or other heating fuels
- Telephone
- House & contents insurance
- Car tax and insurance

Other Non-Discretionary Expenses

These are items that may not be fixed but require regular expenditure:

- Fuel and maintenance for vehicles
- Food
- Clothing
- Public transport
- Household maintenance
- Healthcare products

Semi-Discretionary Expenditure

These are expenses that, while neither luxuries nor essentials, would be difficult to live without. For example:

- Personal care products, e.g. make up
- Haircuts
- Alcohol
- Cinema
- Holidays
- Sports Club memberships

Discretionary Expenditure

"We devised a household budget and forgot to include a clothing allowance!"

And finally we come to items of expenditure that make our lives more fun but we can, if necessary, do without. The list could be many and varied according to our personal tastes and priorities but might include expensive or additional holidays, luxury cars, visits to theatres or health spas, restaurant meals, vintage wines or second homes – whatever floats your boat.

So let's return to our lifestyle pyramid. Try monitoring your expenditure broken down into these categories, and then review your expenditure priorities in the context of your likely level of post-retirement income. You might find that cutbacks and economies in the first two categories allow you to move some expenditure up the pyramid into more discretionary spending on the fun stuff.

Whatever the outcome, the exercise will provide those who have not previously analysed their spending with an early warning alert if their pension incomes are unlikely to allow them to cover their basic overheads, let alone much if any discretionary spending. And if this turns out to be the case, then perhaps a downward adjustment to the overheads – a move to a home that is cheaper to own or releases some capital to bolster your income – could be an answer. Or even a change of utility providers. I hate the phrase, but if you mind the pennies the pounds really will often look after themselves.

Warning – small falls in income mean large falls in the fun stuff

And one final warning. Because a large proportion of the average household's expenditure is used up within the boring fixed overhead categories, a very small change in household income can have a disproportionately dramatic effect on the funds available for discretionary expenditure. Without wishing to labour the point, if 75% of household income disappears in overheads and other essentials, then a 10% fall in net income depresses discretionary spending by 40%. Likewise a 10% rise in the average cost of overheads such as utility bills would depress household discretionary expenditure by 30%. Ouch! What this also demonstrates is that even small errors in our budgeting assumptions can have very painful consequences.

11

How much do we need to save?

'We were well off until our weekly grocery shop yesterday.'

The amounts we save depend to some extent upon the returns that we generate from investing our savings. Returns from the various categories of investments vary over time, but the annual percentage return is less relevant than the 'real' return after taking price inflation into account. If our investment return is less than the rate of inflation, then the value of our investments and the purchasing power of our income will fall. In other words the same money will buy less because prices have risen more quickly than the value of our investments and the income that they generate.

If our investments don't grow faster than inflation then we'll need to save more, but even if our invested savings keep up with inflation, we still need an indication of the total amount of savings that we should aim to accumulate over our working lives through pensions, ISA's or elsewhere.

Let's start with the returns we might expect and with cash – an asset often viewed as the lowest risk investment, although I have argued against this definition in an earlier chapter.

When we published the first edition of the book in 2014, the Bank of England Base Rate was 0.5%. By historical standards this was very low, and with prices of the day to day goods and services that we buy rising at 2.5% each year, if we could generate only 0.5% from our investments, then the value, or 'purchasing power' of our money is falling by 1.5% every year. Cash has not always provided such a low return – in the late 1980's short-term interest rates rose to 15%. This might sound great, but with rampant price inflation the real, inflation adjusted return was a small fraction of this percentage. At the time of writing the Bank of England's Monetary Policy Committee having dropped the ball and watched inflationary pressure build up for over a year before reacting, and base rates are above 5% – but still not far above inflation. So what is the answer?

There is a danger that if we continue to use history as our only guide to the future we will fail to take account of the changes to which I referred in earlier chapters. But we must start somewhere, and sometimes very long-term relationships between asset returns are all that we have to go on, and as I will explain in the course of my descriptions of the various asset categories, if long-term savings are to keep pace with inflation, will need to be exposed to some volatility risk and invested in 'real' assets such as property or equities as opposed to monetary assets such as cash and fixed income bonds.

So even if our investments *do* manage to keep pace with inflation, what is the total value of savings we need to accumulate?

I'm not aware of the existence of a definitive answer to the question of how much we need to save, so we'll use informed guesswork reinforced with the benefit of some years of experience to provide a yardstick. The actuaries among you will be left feeling somewhat queasy at this approach – your profession prefers to base its logic and conclusions on complex arithmetic formulae, but in this case I'm not aware of the existence of a more reliable formula.

I will talk in a later chapter about the importance of how to allocate our savings between the various types of asset, but if we can assume for these purposes that a well spread portfolio of assets can over very long periods allow savers to extract an income of 5% per annum to live on while allowing growth to cater for future price rises, then this is how you might try to come up with a rough guide as to how much you need to save over your working life. Let's start for the moment in today's money and ignore the possible effects of future inflation.

First we need an estimate of the level of income that we are likely to need when we retire. DB schemes typically offer a *maximum* pension of two thirds (66.6%) of a member's final leaving salary, so let's start at two thirds of our *current* salary before deductions for tax, and see if our budget for retirement as described in the previous chapter can be catered for by this level of income:

- Using the 5% income assumption, multiply your target income figure by twenty and you will have an idea of the minimum amount you will need to have saved by the time you stop working.

- Divide this number by the number of years you think you will want to work.

- Divide this number again by twelve to arrive at the monthly saving required.

- Adjust this formula to increase your contributions annually in line with increases in prices and your salary.

The one thing we know for an absolute certainty is that our lives are unlikely to accurately mirror these assumptions, most of which will change regularly over time. But in the absence of anything more scientific, this formula does at least give an indication of the size of the problem and highlights the importance of starting the saving habit at the earliest opportunity.

In case I've lost you, here's an illustration.

Saver A starts putting money aside from the age of 45, while **Saver B** starts at the age of 25. Both want to retire at the age of 65 and their salaries and investment returns are identical:

Saver A

- **Age 45**
- Retirement age 65
- Current salary: £37,500
- Two thirds of current salary: £25,000
- 20x salary total savings target: £500,000
- Assumed annual rate of investment return: 5%
- Annual saving required over 20 years: £15,065
- **Proportion of salary to be saved: 40%**

Saver B

- **Age 25**

- Retirement age 65

- Current salary £37,500

- Two thirds of current salary: £25,000

- 20x salary total savings target: £500,000

- Assumed annual rate of investment return: 5%

- Annual saving required over 40 years: £4,125

- **Proportion of salary to be saved 11%**

Please don't pay too much attention to the specific numbers, but I am comforted that the monthly saving for the 25 year old using these assumptions is 11% of gross salary which feels about right to me, and is not a million miles from a typical company pension scheme's combined annual contribution. However spurious the numbers, these illustrations really do reinforce the necessity to start saving as early as you possibly can, and they show clearly the potential cost of delay.

Before we move on to possible investment strategies, I want to touch briefly on the subject of a pension's ability to provide the best and only savings structure for our retirement needs. We should start with a 'SWOT' analysis:

A Pension's Strengths

- Tax free – contributions are currently made up to a defined level from gross salary before tax is deducted

- A pension's investment returns are not taxed

- Wide range of pension providers and pension structures are available to suit different circumstances

- We cannot access the funds prior to reaching retirement age (currently a minimum of 55 years of age) so we can't blow the money on anything else before then

- The financial regulators provide people who save through approved pensions with some protection against negligence or inappropriate advice

- A 25% tax free cash lump sum can currently be taken from the fund at retirement although this figure is now capped and vulnerable to further changes

Weaknesses

- There is a cap on the annual amount we can save through pensions

- Pensions can be complicated and expensive to administer

- Pensions cannot be drawn or accessed until we're 55

- Income tax is payable as income is paid out

- It is difficult to forecast our post retirement income from DC schemes and it is impossible to forecast future changes to the rules

Threats

- Politicians have seen pensions as a source of additional tax revenue

- Annual maximum contributions continue to be eroded

- Total funding allowances might again be limited (the cap was only recently removed to appease NHS consultants)

- 25% tax free lump sum rule may not last for ever

Opportunities

- There is a wide range of investment products available for pension assets

- Flexibility and tax breaks might one day be improved

- We are no longer forced to buy an annuity at 75 years so there are more investment opportunities for our pension assets post retirement

- Pensions provide some potential inheritance tax planning opportunities

I have resisted the temptation to enlarge on the above because this is not intended as a pensions tutorial. My objective is merely to arm you with questions if you are ever at the mercy of a 'one size fits all' financial advisor.

In most cases the limits to annual contributions and possible future limits to total fund amounts will not prove a constraint, but to increase the Government's tax revenue the amounts that we can put aside tax free each year have fallen inexorably in real, inflation adjusted terms over recent years, and I would not bet against a continuation of this trend. So the costs, inflexibilities and uncertainty over future pensions legislation mean that many feel uncomfortable placing sole reliance on a pension as a savings medium to fund our retirement.

As I will outline in a later chapter covering aspects of taxation, Individual Savings Accounts (ISA's) in particular justify inclusion in our savings matrix. The long term benefits of tax-free income and capital gains and their simplicity and relatively low costs, in my view can *more* than compensate for the absence of the up-front tax relief that we receive on our pension contributions. ISA's also enjoy total flexibility on the age that we can draw an income, and any money withdrawn can be returned to an ISA before the end of the tax year and does not count as an additional contribution.

Although only for the informed and the brave, Enterprise Investment Schemes (EIS's), Seed Enterprise Schemes (SEIS's) and Venture Capital Trusts (VCT's) each have their attractions, but these tax advantaged investments tend to be most appropriate for those concerned with inheritance tax planning and the tax sheltering of very high incomes and protecting capital gains from taxation, because many of these schemes require the acceptance of much higher levels of risk in exchange for their tax breaks.

Now let's move on to the more detailed economics of investment.

12

The Main Categories of Investment Explained

"Long-term, I like bonds; intermediate-term, I like
equities; and short-term, I like scotch."

Before we consider the allocation of assets and how your
advisors might approach the construction of your investment
portfolio in more detail, let's first remind ourselves of the specific
attributes of the main types of investment available to private
investors. Apologies to those of you who are more familiar with
these asset categories, but it is important to start from the most
basic of principles to ensure that our understanding is well
founded.

Cash and Deposits

This category needs little introduction and as I have already explained in the Investment Risk chapter, cash has no liquidity issues (cash *is* liquidity), suffers no volatility, but over extended periods tends to come towards the bottom of the rate-of-return league. At the time of writing, the interest rates available from cash had been negative in real, inflation-adjusted terms, for several years. This means that the returns available from cash, even if you had shopped around for the best rates, can remain substantially below the levels of price inflation for long periods. And remember that over the 50 years before the writing of this book, due to to price inflation the value of £1 in your bank has fallen to little more than 6p!

Gilts and Non-Government bonds

Gilts are debt securities issued by the UK Government as borrowing to pay for government expenditure. The generic term is 'government bonds' but in America these are known as 'Treasuries', or 'Treasury Bills', and in the UK 'Gilts' or 'Gilt Edged Securities'. Investors can buy these bonds, most of which offer investors a fixed rate of interest and mature (are repaid) on a specific date in the future.

Variable rate bonds typically pay interest at a margin over the Bank of England Base Rate and therefore the rate of interest you receive rises or falls to reflect moves in short term interest rates.

Bonds are issued at 'par', typically £1, and repaid at par. It is often possible to find bonds that mature at or around the time when we think that we will need the invested money back in cash, so it enables us to receive a predictable fixed interest rate ('coupon') with the comfort of knowing that our money will be repaid, at par, on that given date.

In normal circumstances (although not at the time of writing!), interest we receive from fixed coupon bonds exceeds the interest rates available from cash deposits, although a bond that is issued with a *very* short maturity date is likely to provide an income much nearer to that of cash than one which is not due for repayment for several years. If we buy a bond and hold it until the borrower redeems (repays) the loan, then we know the *exact* amount of return we will receive over the life of our investment. This is called the yield to redemption or GRY (Gross Redemption Yield).

If we buy a Gilt below par (because rates have risen since the Gilt was issued – as will be described below), the difference between the price we paid and redemption at par (£1) is untaxed. The total *post* tax return from a Gilt – 'Yield to Redemption' can therefore rise for a higher rate tax payer if part of this return is in capital gain.

Bond Pricing

This all seems pretty straightforward until we factor in the likelihood that over the life of a bond, which can be many years or even several decades, inflation and interest rate expectations are likely to change, and investors may wish to trade (sell or buy) their bonds. Although a bond is issued at par and is eventually redeemed at par, it is very unlikely to trade at par for its entire life.

If investors expect interest rates to rise, then they will require a higher yield and will therefore pay less for the bond and may buy bonds *below* the issue price – below par. Conversely, if inflation and interest rate expectations *fall* then investors may be prepared to settle for a lower yield and will be prepared to pay a price *above* par.

All we know for certain is that if we can assume that the borrower will be able to repay the loan at the redemption date, investors who hang on to their bonds until they are redeemed will receive their par value, and therefore as long as the borrower *is* able to repay, the exact returns from a bond is certain and can be calculated at the time of purchase.

Bond yields

A bond's GRY is a calculation of the total combined capital and income return investors will receive if they continue to own the bond until its redemption date. If you buy a bond below par, the GRY will be higher than the coupon because you will gain the difference between the price at which you bought and par. Conversely, if you pay *above* par for your bond, your GRY will be *below* the interest coupon, because you will suffer a loss of the difference between the price you paid and the eventual redemption price at par.

But this does not mean you shouldn't pay a price over par for a bond – the GRY is the GRY, whatever its combination of income and capital gain or loss. For investors who do not mind whether they receive their return in the form of income or a rise in the value of their investment, the price at which you buy a bond is irrelevant, but as described earlier it can be advantageous from a tax perspective to buy bonds – and Gilts in particular – below par.

Credit ratings and risk

Because the risk is considered to be greater, investors usually gain a higher yield when they buy bonds issued by companies than they receive from Gilts, but there are some companies that are considered as safe, or sometimes even safer, than government borrowers, and yields on their bonds are little different to Gilts. These are termed AAA ('triple A') borrowers.

There are several ratings agencies which grade bond issuers according to their analysis and their resulting estimate of the borrowers' capacity to pay the annual interest and repay the debt on the redemption date. The best known is Standard and Poor's, and a borrower's provenance is sometimes referred to as its S&P rating. The highest rating is AAA; it then drops to AA, A, BBB, BB and so on, as the agencies' estimate of risk increases. These credit risk indicators are reviewed regularly and, if necessary, the rating is adjusted to reflect changes in a borrower's perceived ability to service the interest and repay their debts.

The additional yield we receive from non-government bonds is often referred to as their margin over Gilts (or Treasuries in the US) –the extra income we receive for taking the additional credit risk – and this premium is dependent on the borrower's credit rating. The lower the rating, the greater the perceived risk and therefore investors will demand a higher interest rate to compensate.

Maturity date

The other main determinant of yield is a bond's maturity date – in other words, how long the loan is for and when the borrower will repay the bonds' owners at par. You may wonder why this makes such a difference, but it does. In normal circumstances the longer the maturity, the higher the yield. This is because the risk is perceived to be greater.

When I wrote the first edition of 'Feet up by the Pool' in early 2014, short-term interest rates remained *very* low but were expected to with the prospect of a pick up in economic growth and inflation. This expectation is typically factored into the percentage yields available from longer dated bonds that reflect the market's expectations for future inflation and interest rates. Under these circumstances shorter dated bonds would yield less because they will not be around for long enough to enjoy the expected future period of higher interest rates.

Without disappearing too far into the mathematics, even if interest rates were *not* expected to rise in the foreseeable future there are two connected reasons why we would still expect to earn higher interest rates from longer dated bonds. The longer the loan, the greater the risk that the market's expectations for inflation and interest rates will change during the life of the bond. As a result, the price of the bond is likely to be more volatile. Connected to this is the fact that a very small change in the redemption yield requires a larger change in the bond price. This in turn needs to be explained.

The risks and rewards of longer dated bonds

In simple terms, if we buy a bond that pays interest of 5% per annum and will be repaid in five years, and after three years investors are demanding a higher yield, say 6%, the bond price will fall to reflect the fact that over the final two years the bond must provide a yield of 6%. But remember the GRY? The bond will be repaid at par in three years and so if we pay 98p for our bonds then we will make a 2p capital profit and receive three years interest of 5p. Add these two together (its nowhere near as simple as this but let's not worry about the detail) and we have a total return of 17p – three years of 5% income, plus your 2p capital profit – and hey presto, a GRY of around 6% per annum.

Now let's look at a twenty year bond. If after three years investors demand, as in the above example, 6% from a bond with a 5% coupon, then what price will they be prepared to pay for the bond? Because the bond needs to provide a return of 6% for seventeen years as opposed to two in the first example, the bond price required to provide a combined capital and income return (GRY) of 6% over the remaining seventeen years would be 7p lower at approximately 91p. So you can see that the longer dated bond is the more sensitive to changes in future interest rate assumptions.

Why Buy Bonds?

So when should we consider investing in bonds? I referred earlier to the potential to match known liabilities with an asset that provides the maximum return available at the lowest risk. A known liability in 3 years' time is a long time to be sitting in cash with a low return, but too short a period to risk the volatility of shares. So, as my earlier example suggested, why not look for a safe bond that will provide a higher and predictable return but matures, at par, in time to meet the liability?

But surely a long-term saver who is not concerned about volatility or liquidity should not hold bonds? Not necessarily. There have been extended periods when bonds have performed better than assets such as shares and property, so even a 25 year old with a 40 year investment time horizon might be wise on occasions to have some investments in bonds, especially when the world economy has a wobble such as in the aftermath of the 2008 financial crisis when interest rates plummeted, people worried about their jobs, consumer confidence crumbled and for a time it became more difficult for companies to make profits. Government bonds were considered a safe haven and rose in value while equities fell. I have no doubt whatsoever that this could happen again during our lifetimes!

Now, remember the explanation above. What happens to bond prices when investors expect interest rates to fall? They go up. Why do they go up? Because investors will accept the *lower* yield on their investment, and are therefore prepared to pay more and receive a lower GRY.

Bonds – the simple mathematics

My earlier example relating to different maturities covers this issue, but please forgive me for labouring the point. Those readers who have already understood the dynamics of bonds may care to skip the remainder of this section, but some find the relationship between movements in bond prices and bond yields difficult.

When prices rise, yields fall and here's the math's:

We buy a bond for £1. The yield to redemption (GRY) is 5%. This means that if we hold the bond until redemption, the borrower returns our £1 and over the life of the loan pays us 5p every year for each bond we hold. The interest that we receive (the 'running yield') is therefore the same as the GRY because we have bought bonds at par and if we hold it all the way through to the redemption date we are repaid at par and so make neither a capital loss nor gain.

"WHEN BOND YIELD GOES DOWN, CAN YOU EXPLAIN WHY NET ASSET VALUE GOES UP?"

Now let us say that circumstances change during the life of the bond, inflation and interest rates rise and investors now require 10% interest on their bond investments. This might sounds extreme but it has happened – and this comes from the author whose mortgage interest rate rose from 7% to 15% in the space of little over a year when Chancellor Lamont got us thrown out of the European Monetary System in September 1992!

For the purpose of simplicity, let's forget about the more complex GRY and focus on what has to happen to the bond price if the running annual yield moves from 5% to 10%. If we pay only 50p for the same bond then the 5p annual interest payments represent 10% of our purchase price of 50p and so we will receive 10% annual interest on our investment. Conversely if the required yield from the same bond halves to 2.5% then the price we must pay *doubles* to £2 – because 5p is 2.5% of £2.

This arithmetic only works if the bonds are never redeemed; enabling us to ignore the GRY because the bonds will never be redeemed at par, but I hope this simple illustration helps those who struggle to get their heads round the maths.

And while we are on the subject of irredeemables – bonds that will never be repaid – this is typically where the highest yields are available. As the above illustration suggests, these bonds (or Permanent Interest Bearing Shares 'PIBS'), *whoever* issues them – the UK government issued irredeemable Gilts as War Loan to fund the Second World war on the never-never – are riskier than bonds with a final redemption date because they can be much more volatile. This is because these bonds will *never* be redeemed at par and so the bond's price is purely a reflection of the interest rate that investors are happy to accept, and this rate can change very significantly over time, causing large moves in the underlying bond prices.

There is often an additional risk with irredeemables. Banks and building societies have issued irredeemable securities, known as PIBS or PERPS (Permanent Income Baring Shares and Perpetuals) as part of their capital base. Because the bonds are never redeemed, the Bank of England regulators view them as part of the issuer's permanent equity capital. Although the yields are quite sexy, because these securities are typically subordinated, which means that they rank below other creditors and so are the last to be repaid, they should really be viewed as carrying an equity risk so I would strongly recommend that you seek advice before being tempted to buy any.

Equities

Before drilling down into the detail, let's first make sure we understand what ownership of an equity share in a company actually means. In the simplest of terms, a company's shareholders are its owners. After all of the company's costs are paid, interest on loans serviced and taxes are paid, the company's earnings – their net profits after tax – are attributable to its owners – the shareholders. Some, if not all of these profits are usually retained within the company to invest back into the business and fund its future growth, with the balance distributed to its shareholders in the form of dividends.

So let's now compare two investors in the same company: one buys the company's bonds and so in effect buys part of a loan issued by the company, the other invests the same amount of money buying the company's shares. At the end of the year, the bondholder receives interest and the shareholder has the benefit of the net profits after tax. The bondholder is paid first, and only when the company's obligations to their bondholders and any other creditors are satisfied do its shareholders benefit, but of course the bondholder's return is capped at the fixed interest rate on the bond, while the equity return above this is infinite.

I'm sure you know all of this so forgive me, but what happens if the worst happens and the company cannot afford to pay the interest on its loans, let alone dividends to shareholders? Under these circumstances the company's shareholders have no value until bondholders have been repaid in full, so, in extremis, bondholders can force a company to sell assets in order to repay their creditors. Shareholders are at the back of the queue and get whatever is left after all the creditors, including bondholders, have been fully repaid.

Bondholders can also lose all or part of their investment, but under these circumstances the shareholders will get nothing. This is why an understanding of bond ratings is important. If we want to benefit from the higher interest rates available from non-government borrowers, it would seem perverse to lend to a weak borrower and risk losing all of your investment in exchange for a *capped* return, even if the potential return is higher than Gilts.

Given that the majority of us will only ever invest in relatively large, well-diversified companies' shares, the chances of total loss are low, but the principles must be understood, because even large companies can get into difficulties. So why own equities if they can be this risky? I will be looking at how we can construct a diversified investment portfolio in a later chapter, but for now let's stay with the bond comparison to demonstrate why real, as opposed to financial assets, play such a vital role for so many long-term investors.

The Yield Gap, inflation, and the case for investment in equities

You needed to have been around when God was a boy to be familiar with the concept of the yield gap. Like so many such useful perspectives born of the 1960's and 1970's, these simple analytical tools are now considered by many to be simplistic and outdated. They are of course wrong. If we wish to build our understanding from base principles, the relative valuation of bonds and shares is an important historical building block.

Many years ago before the oil price rises of the early 1970's, to compensate investors for their additional risk of loss, the dividend income provided by shares needed to exceed the interest rate from bonds issued by the government. Quite right you might think. Quite wrong as it turned out, and here's why.

Let's assume that we lend the government £1,000 for ten years and so we buy a Gilt which matures in ten years' time. The government issues the Gilt at par, pays interest on the loan annually for ten years and then repays the loan at par. Sounds OK doesn't it? Here's why it isn't even a little bit OK.

When inflation is high, a borrower, not a lender be

The problem was this. Due to a range of factors, including an exponential increase in the price of crude oil in the 1970's, UK price inflation rose to over 10% per annum. An inflation rate of 10% per annum decreases the value of £1 to a little under 35p over ten years. In other words the same £1 coin will only buy 35p's worth of stuff because prices have trebled.

So returning to our £1,000 loan to the government, despite having been repaid our investment of £1,000 we have, in effect, received a sum that will now buy only £350 worth of goods ten years later. A pretty rubbish deal, I hear you say.

The answer is that we needed to be repaid in the same value currency as the one that we lent. Imagine if we had lent money on this basis for twenty years to fund our pension and we suffered 10% inflation over two decades. Then we would only be repaid value of a little over 12p for each pound we had originally lent.

'Real' assets are valued in real money

So why do shares and other 'real' assets such as property provide better protection for the 'real', inflation-adjusted value of our money? In answer to this I make no apology for using another very simple illustration:

Imagine that we buy only one share – in a dairy company – and this dairy sells one product – butter:

- The cost of buying milk and manufacturing the butter is 80p for each pat, and each pat sells for £1.

- The gross profit, before charging fixed overheads, on the sale of every pat of butter is therefore 20p, and after paying rent, office administration and other fixed overhead costs, let us assume that the amount of net profit per pat of butter falls to 10p.

- Of this 10p, the dairy company retains 5p to invest for the future growth of the business, and 5p goes to shareholders as dividend income.

We now have the same ten years of 10% per annum price inflation as I described earlier in relation to Gilts, and all of the dairy's costs rise uniformly by 10% per annum – milk, wages, rent, electricity, everything. Let us further assume that there are no gains in productivity over the decade and so all of the dairy's trading profit margins remain exactly the same.

Let's now redo the sums:

- The cost of buying the milk and manufacturing the butter rises to 207p per pat. Other costs such as rent, interest and taxes rise each year at the same 10% rate from 10p to 26p.

- The total cost is therefore 233p per pat of butter.

- However due to inflation, the sale price of each pat of butter has also risen by 10% per annum to 259p, so the net profit is up from 10p to 26p.

- Again, half is retained and 13p given to shareholders as a dividend.

- So even with zero efficiency gains over the decade, the shareholders' income has risen from 5p to 13p – exactly the amount that they need to compensate for price inflation.

- In the meantime the dairy has invested in a super-duper new factory and more efficient distribution facilities, and so these productivity benefits have decreased the cost per pat by a total of 10% over 10 years to 210p.

- As a result profits rise to 49p and dividends to 24p. Profits and dividends have therefore risen by double the rate of inflation.

Now doesn't that sound a better way to invest our savings and fund our retirement?

So reverting back to the inflationary 1970's, when the market reacted to higher inflation and rebalanced the relative yields between bonds and equities, what happened to this Yield Gap? It became a *reverse* yield gap because investors for the following three decades demanded higher yields from Gilts than from shares to compensate them for this inflation risk.

Then all change again, and fears of deflationary asset and price falls after the financial crisis of 2008 caused a collapse in interest rates to levels which brought them back down *below* the average dividend yield available from company shares. So here we were over 40 years on from the oil crises of the 1970's, back with a yield gap, but as the economy recovered and inflation pressures eventually re-emerged, we did not have to wait too long before it reversed again and Gilt yields now at the time of writing exceed the average yields from equities.

The dairy illustration might appear simplistic but it does provide an accurate illustration of the case for using real assets to fund real, inflation-adjusted long-term incomes. If price inflation is to continue then the argument for investing in assets such as shares and property is compelling. I include property for two main reasons – firstly like equities, earnings from rents and asset values tend to increase with inflation, and second, many investors feel comfortable with the tangible and understandable nature of property.

Convertibles

A convertible bond or convertible preference share is a hybrid security that combines some of the attributes of both bonds and equities. Like bonds, convertibles typically provide a fixed rate of annual interest but are convertible into shares in the issuing company. When issued, convertibles normally yield more income than the dividends from an equivalent investment in the company's shares, but this is compensated by a conversion premium – the fact that the price at which the convertible can be exchanged for shares is higher than the current share price at the time of issue. In normal circumstances, the higher the yield differential between the convertible and the shares, the larger the conversion premium.

On the face of it convertibles can provide a mixture of higher immediate income than the underlying equity and potential for future growth if the equity price exceeds the level at which the convertible can switch into the equity and can therefore serve a useful purpose in a diversified portfolio. However the flip side is that whenever I've bought a convertible I look back and see that I would have been better off buying either shares or the bonds. If the shares do well I've missed a significant proportion of their growth, but if the shares do poorly and I end up never converting (because the share price never reaches the conversion price), then I should have bought a higher yielding bond. In the UK new convertible issues are now very rare, probably because demand for them is limited.

Private Equity

Private equity is sometimes referred to as either venture capital or unquoted equity and is a term for equity investments in companies whose shares are not listed on a stock exchange.

Just because a share is not quoted or listed on a recognised stock exchange does not of itself make it riskier than a listed share. Yes, there may be the risk of a lack of liquidity and the ability to sell, but many smaller *quoted* companies are also very difficult to buy and sell and brokers often need to work hard to find a buyer at a discount – or seller at a premium price – if we wish to trade their shares.

So the *underlying* risk of investing in private equity can be no different to a share listed on a recognised stock exchange – risk is dependent upon the nature of the underlying business. However the term 'venture capital' has become synonymous with higher risk investments and implies that the investment opportunity comes at a time when the company is at an early stage in its development when the risk of failure and loss is at its greatest.

Development capital is often required at a later stage to fund a company's growth when the business case is proven, and often exposes investors to a lower level of risk than early stage venture capital. It can be some years, if ever, that a successful start-up venture gets to the point of and Initial Public Offering (IPO) and becomes listed and traded on a recognised stock exchange. Many successful private companies see little advantage to be gained from a listing, and so remain private, and their shareholders typically realise their investment via a sale to another investor or an industry buyer.

Early stage financing is where the risks and rewards from private equity can be the greatest, and both institutions and private investors typically gain their exposures to this area of private equity through the plethora of funds available, some of which are themselves very large and several are quoted on recognised exchanges which of course addresses the issue of liquidity. The assumption behind an investment in a venture capital fund is that it only takes a small number of successes to offset the inevitability that many new ventures do not succeed. Many later stage development capital or 'pre IPO' funds are associated with a very much lower risk of loss because the businesses in which these funds invest are already proven.

One more comment from someone who has been involved in the private equity sector for much of the latter part of my working career. In the earlier equity section, I refer in a later chapter to the regular and detailed information made available by the larger listed companies, but suggest that one of the reasons for considering the use of collective funds for our smaller companies' exposure was that small companies' reporting requirements are less onerous and so there is less publicly available information on which to base our investment decisions.

Managers of private equity investments hear from the management teams in their companies and see their trading numbers weekly and sometimes daily. This often facilitates earlier questioning and subsequent action than could ever be possible with a quoted company investment where the listing rules and financial regulations that govern their communications with advisors and shareholders are very much more restrictive. Even so, although investing over long periods into the private equity sector has been rewarding and has justified the additional risks, professional advice is an essential requirement for all but the most experienced investors.

Property

Many large pension funds invest directly in property. Residential housing tends not to represent much, if any, of their property exposure and much of it is invested on the basis of rental yield and typically concentrated in commercial sectors such as offices, shops, and industrial units such as factories and warehouses. As I suggested earlier, property enjoys many of the attributes of equities, but direct investment into individual buildings can represent a sizeable commitment, often too large for private individuals to achieve the necessary spread of risk.

Property also suffers from a lack of liquidity, so is strictly for the long-term investor. Smaller private investors buy their property exposures through collective funds or listed property shares in companies (Real Estate Investment Trusts or 'REITS') that own and manage large numbers of properties. This allows investors to spread their risk over a large number of individual properties so as not to be reliant on the rents and value of a single building. As importantly, like any other listed share, property shares allow investors to buy and sell our property investments easily and cheaply.

Property investments combine some of the attributes of both bonds and equities. Investors buy commercial properties on the basis of their rental yield – the annual income they receive from renting the property to a tenant for the period of a lease. As a result, the reliability of the tenant and the length of time the tenant is contractually committed to paying the rent offers similar characteristics to a bond, the difference being at the end of the lease, when instead of receiving a *cash* repayment, the investor may have an empty property to redevelop, refurbish or re let.

The other main difference from bond investments is the typical periodic 'upward only' rent reviews when rents can rise, and so the investor's income and asset values can rise and offer protection against inflation if their tenants remain able to pay the rent. It is in this way that property investments share some of the characteristics of an equity. Property is such a huge and diverse asset class I will not even attempt to do it justice here, and I have confined my comments to some of its overall generic characteristics and will return later to consider how it might fit into a diversified portfolio of investments.

Hedge Funds

Hedge funds is an investment category that really does require some clarification. For a start the title is positively misleading. The term 'hedge fund' covers a multitude of sins but my understanding of the word 'hedged' brings with it an assumption that there is some form of insurance against or mitigation of risk. Doesn't the phrase 'hedge your bets' suggest a conservative approach? I'm sure that those originally responsible for the title had exactly this in mind but many (but by no means all) of those who now claim to inhabit the hedge fund sector have very different and less risk-averse investment strategies. Perhaps the term 'Alternative Strategies' provides a more accurate description of the sector.

I am of course being a little unfair, but I am determined not to allow facts to get in the way of my long held prejudice, so please take my cynicism with a pinch of salt because there are of course plenty of hedge fund managers who are not only very talented but are also successful in managing the level of investment risk. However, before I get carried away with such moderate thoughts let's get back to the prejudice.

In my experience, hedge funds are sometimes presented as the Holy Grail of generating high, equity-like returns but at a risk more associated with the relative safety of bonds. In other words these ingenious fund managers can develop complex investment techniques that provide high returns without commensurately high levels of volatility or correlation with equity returns. To be fair, much of the sector's marketing is focused on funds of hedge funds which provide a wide spread of individual and diverse strategies in one fund, which can indeed help to mitigate risk.

Modern Portfolio Theory

So here is the theory – in fact here is a simple guide to Modern Portfolio Theory, an approach that is not confined to funds of hedge funds, but is often used in the context of investment products that invest in a range of hedge funds, known as funds of funds.

The buzzword is 'correlation'. Correlation between assets is the extent to which changes in economic or political circumstances affect different assets differently. The theory goes that you can take more risk, and gain more reward, by investing in a range of individual investment strategies that perform differently from one another under the same market conditions.

Here is a very simplistic example of potential non-correlation to which I have already referred – bonds and shares:

- The economy moves into recession, business activity falls, company profits fall, as do their share prices.

- Inflation falls and The Bank of England brings interest rates down in order to stimulate the economy, bond yields fall and so bond prices rise.

Under these circumstances bonds and shares will have shown a *negative* correlation because they have moved in opposite directions under the same economic conditions.

Some hedge fund managers develop complex strategies to achieve this effect, using a wide variety of different asset types or derivatives, some so complex and esoteric that I can't even begin to understand them myself let alone explain them here. But I will

"We've changed our investment strategy."

spend a little bit of time explaining a hedge fund's simplest and most common measure of risk – Standard Deviation. I would have a high degree of sympathy if you've already lost interest in hedge funds and want to skip to the next chapter, but for those gluttons for further punishment who are determined to bat on, welcome to the theory of Normal Distribution.

Standard Deviation – a measure of volatility

Standard Deviation is a measure of volatility risk. For those already familiar with the concept and use of normal distribution statistics then this isn't for you, but potential investors in hedge funds do need to understand that the higher the measure of Standard Deviation, the greater the fund's historic volatility.

One Standard Deviation either side of the mean will, if the distribution is 'normal', contain around two thirds of the historic outcomes. So if the average annual return from shares has been, say, 8%, and the Standard Deviation is 8%, then in two years out of every three, if history is an effective guide to the future, then the annual return can expected to be between zero and 16%, 8% either side of the mean, and in over nine out of every ten of years we should expect the outcomes to be within *two* standard deviations either side of the mean – i.e. between minus 16% and plus 24%.

Now let us assume that bond investments have historically provided a mean annual return of 4% at a Standard deviation of 3%, then we might expect to see returns between 1% and 7% in two years out of three, and between minus 2% and plus 10% in over nine years out of every ten. If we use this measure as a quantum of risk, we can conclude that bonds provide lower returns but are less volatile. 'Big deal' I hear you say and yes, it looks obvious, but when the technique is used to measure the volatility of a wider range of assets and strategies it can provide more interesting, useful and sometimes unexpected conclusions.

So let's get back to funds of hedge funds, constructed by specialist managers and analysts to provide this Holy Grail of high returns with low risk by matching uncorrelated assets and investment strategies. Sounds great, and prior to the financial crash in 2008 many traditionally risk-averse investors, such as Lloyd's insurance companies, found it a difficult story to resist, particularly at a time when the interest rates that they relied on to provide returns on their capital were negligible and monetary assets were providing such desultory returns. You probably know how it all ended, but here's why.

The statistics behind risk and correlation analysis are by their nature historic. As a result, these techniques assume that the past is a useful and reliable guide to the future, and this has very often been the case. However I there are events that have cause investment markets to cease operating with any degree of efficiency, liquidity or predictability, sometimes for several months after an economic or financial shock – and in some cases for several years.

History doesn't *always* repeat itself

The 1970's oil crisis, Sterling's expulsion from the European Monetary System in 1992, the 'dot com' technology boom and bust in 2000 and the banking crises of the early 1970s' and 2008 have all caused financial markets to behave in unpredictable ways and, just as importantly for many hedge fund strategies, liquidity has dried up and it has become almost impossible to trade or hedge risk in the immediate aftermath.

Such events can destroy what had previously appeared to be sound and stable long-term performance track records and with them the credibility of their managers and strategies, because some hedge funds' strategies became inoperable and stopped working until their markets returned to normality. So historical risk analysis cannot always cope with economic shocks in a volatile and ever changing world.

So *before* the 2008 financial crash many funds of funds salesmen maintained that due to their funds' diverse and uncorrelated investment strategy, if stock markets fell 25%, their funds would fall by only 10% and would recover these losses within six months. You may be aware of the reality. Some funds fell very dramatically in value and not all recovered. Ever. To add insult to injury, some funds locked their investors into their investments for several years before they could redeem them for cash. But allow me to end this section on a more up-beat note by giving an example of a popular and effective strategy used by many hedge fund managers to back their analytical skills while excluding much of the risk of investing in the underlying market.

'Long/short' investing – Alpha vs. Beta

The returns from portfolios of equity investments are often split into two constituent parts, characterised as Alpha and Beta. Beta is the extent to which individual shares have historically reflected moves in the overall stock market. A Beta of more than one shows that a share has in the past moved further up *or* down, than the overall market index. If the share's Beta has been *less* than one, then the shares have historically risen or fallen by less than the market index as a whole.

Alpha is a measure of how much of the performance of a portfolio of shares has been attributable to the strategy and stock picking ability of the manager as opposed to merely reflecting moves in the overall market – the 'beta'.

A long/short strategy removes some or all of the market risk and can leave the investor with an exposure confined to alpha – the stock picking ability of the fund managers selecting the shares for the fund.

Shares that the manager believes will underperform are 'shorted', which means the fund's manager sells shares that it does not own in the hope that it can buy the shares back at a lower absolute or relative price. Don't worry about how this is done; just believe me that it can be – by borrowing someone else's shares and then selling them.

Shares that the manager believes will perform best are bought, so the fund is 'long' of these shares. The net result is that if the 'longs' do better than the 'shorts', the investor will make money without much if any exposure to the equity market's underlying movements. Often the 'longs' and 'shorts' are not perfectly matched, but the technique offers another tool to hedge fund managers that can enable them to back their judgment while decreasing the portfolios' overall volatility.

Should a diversified investment portfolio include hedge funds?

Personally I own no hedge funds, not because of any inbuilt prejudice but because I struggle to get comfortable with investing in strategies that I do not fully understand. Many fund of funds managers have generated consistently high returns, but when one of the best known and oft consulted lady fund managers in the

"I'm looking for a hedge against my hedge funds."

UK invested over 10% of her fund of hedge funds into Bernie Maddorf's scam which enabled his hedge fund to systematically steal investors' money, then I'm afraid I finally lost the faith. How anyone with her reputation and experience in fund management can invest in a 'strategy' that they could not possibly have even *begun* to understand I cannot fathom. We now know that the strategy was to defraud investors, steal their money and buy yachts and private jets with the proceeds.

We shouldn't discount the use of hedge funds, but the selection process needs to be handled with extreme care, and please don't follow the crowd into opaque 'black box strategies' which rely on complex computer programs, even if they appear successful. If it looks too good to be true then guess what, it very often *is*. Stick to transparent strategies that you and your advisors can properly analyse understand and explain.

If I can offer a more useful definition of a hedge fund that deserves investigation, then it is a fund that offers an environment and the flexibility for an outstanding fund manager to exercise his or her skills to provide consistently high returns for investors, and whose performance related fee structure offers the managers the incentive of an appropriate share of the fund's performance. If you are ever advised to invest in hedge funds then perhaps this could provide a benchmark against which to question the recommendation.

International Investments

The penultimate section in this chapter relates to the use of non-domestic investments to provide better performance and a greater spread of risk. So with such a broad range of domestic investment opportunities available, why should we consider investing in foreign markets? Here is a list of some possible reasons:

- To gain exposure to countries with economies growing faster than ours

- To gain exposure to industries not represented in our domestic market

- To spread and diversify economic risk

- To spread and diversify political risk

There are ways in which we can achieve *all* of these benefits without investing directly into overseas equity markets. For instance companies such as Unilever provide diversified exposures to fast growing economies through their sales of cooking oils and soaps and other consumer products into emerging economies, and we should recognise that a high proportion of the earnings from many large companies listed on the London Stock Exchange are derived from overseas subsidiaries and therefore themselves provide exposure to overseas markets and a range of currencies. Current estimates suggest that upwards of 70% of the earnings of the FTSE 100 Index shareware derived from outside the UK and are not earned in Sterling.

There are even some overseas companies who choose to list on the London Stock Exchange and can be purchased as part of a UK equity portfolio. These include mining and resources companies in particular. But even of those companies that do not have significant operations overseas, many export their products and services and therefore still provide investors with some of the benefits of overseas diversification. However the four largest listed companies in the world are listed on the American Nasdaq Index (the National Association of Securities Dealers Automated Quotations) account for such a large proportion of the world's combined equity markets that they cannot be ignored. Apple, Amazon, Alphabet and Microsoft at the time of writing account for nearly 40% of the Index with a combined valuation of more than double that of all the companies listed on the London Stock Exchange. Since starting on this edition another share has blasted through into this category-Nvidia which is seen as a major beneficiary of the dramatic development of Artificial Intelligence.

Investment trusts, investment companies and funds also offer effective ways of achieving exposure to foreign shares and even specific industry sectors, both here and abroad. These investment vehicles offer a spread of specific share risk by holding a large number of underlying investments selected by specialists in the geographic area or industry sector. More on this later.

So in summary, companies quoted on the London stock exchange and London listed investment funds already offer a wide range of exposures to overseas markets, removing the necessity and expense of buying individual foreign investments in their domestic stock markets.

Globalisation

The growing interdependence of countries' economies and, more specifically, the growth of trade between developed and developing nations, means that the diversification benefits from investing overseas are perhaps more limited than they once were. There is a saying that if the American economy sneezes, then the rest of the world catches a cold, and the same can now be said of China.

The development of trade between countries means that their economies have become increasingly inter-dependent, and so the health of one country's economy can greatly affect its trading partners, and economic conditions within the larger economic regions can have global effects. For example, the UK is not a member of the Eurozone but was still heavily exposed to the effects of the recession in Continental Europe that followed the Euro currency crisis.

The trend towards increased globalisation has however taken a knock following the pandemic and the war in Ukraine. Both events have highlighted the risks to nations that have become over-reliant on overseas suppliers of strategically important products and services. If the UK had not itself secured supplies of Covid vaccines, reliance on European and American providers would have threatened the essential vaccine rollout, and war in Ukraine has demonstrated the importance of self-sufficiency in food and fertilisers which proved irreplaceable in the short term and led to soaring food price inflation.

Currencies

If we decide to explore the benefits of diversification into overseas markets we will also be exposed to an additional currency risk. This is the risk that the translation of the value of our overseas investments can change when the exchange rates between the respective currencies move.

For instance, we could enjoy a 10% return from an investment in the local currency but can lose this return, and more, if the domestic currency of the investment falls 10% or more when translated back into Pounds. Likewise, domestic companies with operations and earnings overseas can find their profits affected by currency movements when these profits are translated back into Sterling. Of course if the rate of exchange between the pound and other currencies falls and the pound weakens, then we enjoy an *increase* in our total return when we translate the value back into pounds.

So, should we worry about currency movements? There is a school of thought that suggests that if we invest overseas to gain exposure to faster growing economies, then the currencies of these countries should be strong and so would therefore enhance our Sterling returns. In other more 'mature' economies it is a more difficult judgment, but on balance I believe that some of the diversification benefits we gain from investing overseas are enhanced by the fact that we are exposed to other currencies.

This is particularly relevant for the diversification of political risk – the risk that the UK finds itself governed by a less business and capitalist-friendly administration that might threaten to undermine the prospects for businesses operating and taxed in the UK. Under these conditions the trading performance and less competitive exports could be expected to weaken pound relative to other currencies, and this is when the diversification of risk from investing in companies with a significant proportion of earnings from outside the UK, or into overseas shares, would prove particularly rewarding.

For investors who wish to remove currency risk altogether from their exposures to overseas assets, it is possible to find funds that cover the currency exposure back into Sterling, thereby removing this risk altogether. This requires the selling of the overseas currency exposure either through forward currency sale contracts or the use of currency options, neither of which I need explain here but both can provide efficient and sometimes cost effective ways of converting the underlying investment return back into Sterling. Remember that as a UK resident your expenses will be mainly Sterling based, so investment returns will eventually need to be returned to your domestic currency.

Finally, before I leave the subject of currencies I should just touch on currency funds. These are funds that inhabit the hedge fund sector that trade between currencies, using movements between currencies to generate trading profits. This type of trading activity, whether in currencies or any other commodity, is sometimes recommended as part of a diversification strategy on the basis that the returns are a function of the manager's trading skill and therefore not correlated to movements in their other investments. Personally I can see no other justification for investing in a currency fund. The results are, by definition, a gamble on the skills of the traders and there is no long-term investment rationale or justification for any fund whose performance cannot be predicted and provides no obvious match for any future liability.

13

How to Value Companies
and their Shares

AND WHEN WERE YOU PLANNING ON TELLING ME
THAT THE DOG HAD INVESTED IN FACEBOOK?

Most of us consider the value of our possessions to be the price at which the items can either be sold or replaced. Some shares are no different. Items such as jewellery and property can be valued with the benefit of the expert opinion of an independent professional valuer and, likewise, some shares that trade on the basis of their underlying asset values. For example, shares such as property companies or investment trusts have independently verified Net Asset Values based on the combined individual values their underlying investments, and in the case of investment trusts that

122

invest in listed equities, at the end of each day the combined values of all of their investments is calculated and this enables investors to know the exact underlying asset value of their shares the following morning.

Trading companies also own assets but these are often not an investor's prime consideration when valuing their shares, because it is the income and profits that these assets and resources can generate for the shareholders that determine a trading company's value. The company might own machinery, cars, buildings, computers and office furniture but these are merely the tools that they need in order to generate income, make profits and pay dividends, and although assets are important for the operation of the business – and are itemised and valued in the company's balance sheet, it is the company's trading prospects that determine its value.

There are two basic fundamental measures of a share's value: earnings multiple and the dividend yield. There is no one individual that decides on the correct valuation of a company's shares, but influential analysts and guidance from the companies themselves do influence the combined views of the thousands of investors who buy and sell shares quoted on the stock markets and thereby determine the price.

In the short-term a company's share price valuation is merely a function of supply and demand for its shares – the balance between buyers and sellers on a particular day. It is often a change in the outlook for a company, or some unexpected development leading to a change in future profit expectations that changes that balance between buyers and sellers and moves a share's price up or down relative to its index or its peers. After unexpected good or bad news, there is likely to be an imbalance of investors wishing to buy or sell, and the share price value will rise or fall to a level at which a balance between buyers and sellers returns and the share price will stabilise at the new valuation level.

Relative vs. Absolute Values

You will often see valuations or movements in share prices described as 'relative', and this needs to be explained. Movements of the overall stock market reflect the change in the value of the weighted average of every company, meaning that every constituent is represented in the proportions that they individually represent of the overall index. This average is therefore made up of many individual company shares representing a wide variety of industries and, as such, is subject to differing influences that will effect investor sentiment toward a company's shares. Investors in the stock market are trying to select shares that are likely to perform as well, or better than, the average, so their focus is on the share's expected return *relative* to the index, as opposed to just the 'absolute' return from the share itself. The absolute return is the actual monetary amount that the shares generate through dividend income and capital gain.

This might seem counter-intuitive – surely we only care about the return, not whether the return, good or bad, up or down, is better or worse than this average? Well yes of course we do, but if we have taken a long-term decision to commit some of our savings to equities, then this decision was made on the assumption that over long periods *real* assets such as company shares do a good job at protecting the value of our investments from the effects of inflation. So a focus on relative performance assumes that we are already committed to the concept of equity investment and so our focus is then on trying to select and hold the shares that will do 'relatively' well when compared with the market as a whole. If successful, investors can generate alpha – a return that exceeds the index. Many investors who do not want to risk their investments performing *less* well than the index as a whole can buy index funds which exactly match the index return.

We value a trading company on the basis of a multiple of what it earns

To arrive at a company's earnings per share we divide its annual net profit after tax by the total number of shares in issue. We then divide the share price by the earnings per share and that gives us the company's earnings multiple.

For example:

- Company A has post-tax profits of £10 million
- There are 10 million shares in issue.
- The company's earnings per share are therefore £1.
- If the company's share price is £10 then the earnings multiple is 10x

Now in isolation this earnings multiple or Price Earnings Ratio ('PE') tells us relatively little about the share's value – is 10x cheap or expensive? We must now compare this valuation against the average for *all* shares and also against other shares in the company's industrial sector. The former shows us whether the shares are relatively cheap or expensive when compared with other shares in the market, the latter how the company is valued relative to other companies that operate in the same industry sector.

Let us assume that the average multiple for the entire stock market is 13x earnings and Company A's industry sector has an average multiple of 9x, what should we conclude? For some reason the market is valuing this sector more cheaply than the average for all shares, but Company A, valued at 10x earnings, is valued more highly than the average for its industry sector.

Rather than continue with this hypothetical example, we need to explore the reasons why some companies and some industry sectors are valued more highly than others. Companies with above average multiples are often valued highly because their earnings are expected to grow faster than the average. This would result in the earnings multiple falling in future years. For example:

- *Company B's shares trade at a price which represents earnings multiple of 15x and so appears to be more expensively valued than the average share in the stock market.*

Using the same earnings numbers that we used for Company A, let's now apply Company B's higher multiple:

- *Company B has post-tax profits of £10 million,*

- *Company B has 10 million shares in issue and so has earnings per share of £1.*

- *But company B trades at £15 which represents a 15x multiple of its earnings.*

So why would investors be prepared to pay a higher price for company B if this year's profits are the same as Company A's and pay 15x earnings when the share market as a whole trades at a lower earnings multiple of 13x? A company's market value is typically based on investors' and analysts' combined assumptions relating to its *future* profits, known as prospective earnings, rather than its current or historic earnings.

So let's now look at the forecast profits for the next three years' Earnings Per Share (EPS) and the resulting Price: Earnings Ratios (PER) using today's share prices:

	Share Price.	Yr1 EPS.	Yr1 PER.	Yr2 EPS.	Yr2 PER.	Yr3 EPS	Yr3 PER
Company A.	£10	£1.00	10x.	£1.05	9.5x	£1.10	9x
Company B.	£15	£1.00	15x.	£1.30	11.5x	£1.70	8.8x

From this example you can see why company B was rated so highly, because investors believed that its forecast future profits growth justified paying a higher multiple of today's earnings, and on the basis of the Year 3 forecast the company's shares look relatively cheap.

Now if both Company A and Company B continue to trade on their current earnings multiples of 10x and 15x respectively, their share prices would rise in line with their earnings:

- Year 3 Company A share price 10x £1.10 = £11.00
- Year 3 Company B share price 15x £1.70 = £25.50

Rerating – what can change the relative valuation of a share?

On the basis of the above analysis we can see why the market might apply a higher valuation to Company B, but as well as the short term growth prospects for a company's earnings, investors are also influenced by the quality of earnings.

By 'quality' we mean the predictability and sustainability of earnings that offer investors the confidence that not only will these forecasts be achieved, but the performance is also sustainable over a longer period.

If Year 3 represents the peak earnings that Company B is likely to produce and that it's growth could slow or even cease thereafter, then the market is likely to 'de-rate' the shares. If investors are concerned that Year 3 earnings are not sustainable or that Company B's previously strong growth is likely to slow down, then they may only be prepared to value Company B at 8x the expected Year 3 earnings and the share price would therefore only rise to £13.60, which represents 8x earnings of £1.70.

If investment analysts forecast that Company A, after years of pedestrian growth, was about to grow much faster after Year 3 and this led to investors 're-rating' the shares to a valuation multiple of 15x, causing the price to rise to £16.50, 15x earnings of £1.10. So despite Company A's relatively pedestrian growth over the short term, its shares could actually perform better than Company B's because its longer-term growth prospects have improved.

The examples above are only intended to show that it is changes in expectations for future earnings that move individual share prices relative to the market or it's piers, rather than current or historic earnings, and the more stable and predictable a company's long term growth prospects, the higher their likely earnings multiple. Before the dramatic fall in the US Nasdaq Index in 2022, shares such as Amazon, Netflix and Microsoft were trading on PE's offer 50x and we saw the size and speed of falls in highly valued shares when the economic background changes and threatens their future growth. In this case it was rising inflation and interest rate which made the returns from lower risk investments such as cash more attractive.

Before we move on to the second important valuation criteria we should consider the attributes of a company's shares that might affect it's rating by the market, and why share prices might suffer downward valuations by the market or benefit from an upward re-ratings. As we can see from the examples above, investors are richly rewarded for investing in companies whose earnings grow steadily and whose share price multiples of earnings remain stable or improve.

The 'quality' of Earnings

Let's start with earnings quality – the sustainability and predictability of earnings growth. There are some excellent companies that operate in unpredictable areas. Cyclical industries such as mining, property development, some areas of manufacturing and luxury goods manufacturers and retailers are sectors whose fortunes tend to fluctuate in line with the economic environment and our disposable incomes. Compare these industries with food manufacturers and retailers, pharmaceutical and utility companies whose products and services are essential non-discretionary purchases and business prospects tend not to be so badly affected by economic slowdowns and pressure on household incomes. We might expect the volatility and relatively unpredictable nature of the former to depress their long-term share ratings.

Before moving on from this point, we should also note that companies within a sector such as food retailers can have very different experiences when times are tough. For instance, following the 2008 financial crisis consumer incomes were under pressure with prices in the shops rising much faster than average pay, and the prime beneficiaries were discount retailers such as Lidl and Aldi who benefited at the expense of the larger traditional stores, whose market shares fell as customers deserted them for lower priced discount food stores.

Finally, let's list some of the attributes which we might seek if we are looking for shares that are more likely to provide sustainable long-term returns and achieve the highest earnings multiples:

- Companies with predictable and sustainable sources of earnings from non-cyclical industries

- Companies with limited exposure to any single source of income

- Companies with exposure to products and services with long term growth potential

- Companies benefitting from fundamental change such as climate change or new technological revolutions such as Artificial Intelligence (AI)

- Companies with customers from a wide range of geographic areas

This list is neither exhaustive nor is it intended to suggest that companies that do not meet these criteria are likely to underperform or trade at lower multiples than those that do. There are periods during the economic cycle when cyclical companies perform much better than less cyclical growth businesses, and there are equally opportunities to benefit from fast growing technology companies exposed to the success of specific new product developments such as Apple. But such opportunities, while being potentially very rewarding, can require a more active approach to equity investment than a strategy focused on more diversified or predictable companies without the same capacity for surprises – good or bad – or the danger of new products and technologies developed by competitors.

Earnings Yields and Dividends

A company's earnings yield is the percentage return that its shareholders would receive if it was to pay out all of its earnings in annual dividends.

Returning to the examples above:

- *Company A earned £1 which was an earnings yield of 10% of its £10 share price*

- *Company B also earned £1 but on a share price of £15 this only represented an earnings yield of 6.6%.*

Few companies pay out all of their earnings because some of their earnings need to be reinvested in the future growth of the business, but the earnings yield calculation does at least offer a consistent measurement yardstick.

Dividend Yields

Dividends are an important constituent of equity returns, not only because the income from our investments makes a significant contribution to our total return, but because once the dividend payment is in our bank account it is ours, while a paper profit on our shares is only crystallised when we sell. But in the context of our pensions, the most important aspect of all is the ability of a diversified portfolio of shares to provide an income which rises to compensate for the increasing cost of living.

Many of the issues relating to the growth and sustainability of dividends reflect the same dynamics as we covered in relation to earnings multiples – increased earnings are typically a prerequisite for increasing dividends. But we must be aware of some of the related issues that affect the quantity and sustainability of a company's annual dividend payments and these can relate to dividend cover.

Dividend Cover

A company's earnings yield is calculated on the basis that all the earnings are paid out to shareholders, but if this were to be the case then any temporary fall in earnings might be expected to decrease the sums paid out to shareholders in dividends. So the level of dividend cover – the proportion of a company's earnings that are paid out to shareholders in dividends – is an important factor in investors' perceptions of the sustainability of the income that they receive, and if they are living off their dividend income this is a very important factor. For example:

- **Company A** earns £1 per share and pays an annual dividend of £1 per share

- **Company B** earns £1 per share and pays an annual dividend of 50p per share

- **Company C** earns 50p per share and pays an annual dividend of £1 per share

Company A pays out 100% of its earnings so its dividend is 1x covered.

Company A might have decided to pay out all of its earnings for any number of reasons, including:

- management can see no attractive opportunities to invest the money back into the company to generate future growth, so decide to return profits to shareholder through dividends

- the company already has ample reserves to invest for future growth

- the company's business is structured specifically to generate maximum income for its investors, for example an investment trust

- the company usually pays a well-covered dividend, but this year profits fell. However, as they are expected to recover next year, the directors see little advantage in irritating shareholders by cutting their dividend. The maintenance or increase in the dividend gives the market a strong indication of the Board's confidence in the business's future prospects

Company B pays out 50% of its earnings, and so its dividend is 2x covered – a not untypical policy for a company to follow, paying shareholders a reasonable and sustainable dividend while retaining half its earnings for future investment in the business

Company C pays out double what it earned, and so the dividend is only 50% covered by earnings.

So why would a company pay out more than it earned?

- as with Company A the Board might be confident that this year's earnings were only temporarily depressed and can be expected to recover to enable a covered dividend to be paid next year

- companies such as banks and insurance companies often need to retain significant reserves against one-off liabilities such as fines or bad debts in the case of banks, or reserves against future claims following a natural disaster in the case of insurance companies. Although these reserves are charged against profits, the cash can sometimes remain in reserves for some years before the payments are required, so if the Board considers that the underlying earnings performance, stripping out the one-off reserving, justifies maintaining the dividend, even if the company has made a loss the dividend could be paid from the companies retained reserves.

Companies usually cut their dividends only as a last resort, and at their peril. Shareholders can take many years to forgive and forget – unless there is a very obvious and unavoidable justification. This is another reason why some companies continue to pay uncovered dividends long after they should have taken the tough decision to retain all of their available resources for the sake of the business's future, and to accept the inevitable short term fall in their share's valuation as those who wish to maintain their income are forced to sell shares in order to buy their income elsewhere. Interest rate rises in 2022 led both to write-downs in the values of property values and profits squeezed as interest rates payable on companies' debt exceeded increases in their rental income resulting in dividends uncovered by profits.

The outlook for earnings and dividends are important drivers of value. Get the earnings and dividend forecasts and assumptions right, and over the long-term the capital values will look after themselves.

14

Investment Funds and Management Fees

"On the contrary, the fund's performance has
been quite good when viewed in dog's years."

Now that we've covered the main categories of investment readily
available to private investors, I feel it is important to cover some
of the collective fund structures that are available, when they
might be appropriate, and the fees that they charge.

First, I need to explain the use for which these funds are designed and the differences between closed end investment trusts and open ended unit trusts and companies.

When should we consider investing through funds?

- When we cannot achieve a sufficient spread of risk via direct investments.

  There are commissions and other costs incurred when we buy and sell shares, and in particular the minimum commission rates charged by stockbrokers that can make small purchases of shares and bonds very expensive. Moreover, if you only wish to commit a small amount of money to an investment sector or country's stockmarket, funds provide cost effective diversification through a spread of risk across a large number of underlying holdings.

- Funds are simple and easy to administer.

  Buying a fund is the equivalent of buying an individual share but can offer a sufficient underlying spread of investment risk to prevent the requirement to diversify by buying a range of different individual shares. An investor in funds could have fewer individual investments to monitor and administer.

- Funds provide access to expertise in specific markets sectors e.g. resources, technology or property.

  Even institutions and the most experienced private investors often resort to the use of funds to gain exposures to industry sectors where they either require specialist expertise, such as mining or technology, or where they wish to allocate relatively small amounts of their capital that are too difficult and costly to invest directly into a spread of underlying investments.

- Funds can provide broadly spread access to overseas markets.

An allocation to fast growing developing economies requires specialist expertise. Some funds provide exposure to a range of different markets in a region such as. South East Asia – where it would be impossible for most private investors to achieve a sufficient spread of individual shares to diversify their risk.

- Funds offer small investors access to successful fund managers.

Partly due to their administration costs and management fees, the majority of fund managers struggle to consistently outperform the market indices into which they invest, although as I mentioned under the hedge fund section, there are some outstanding managers who provide notable exceptions to this rule.

Although very rare, there can be instances where the individual stock selections of the best managers can be as rewarding as the optimum asset allocation between the different markets, but when we decide to use funds, it is very much more important to select the right markets and industry sectors than the star manager, because it has historically been the asset allocation rather than the selection of the individual underlying investments that generates by far the largest differentiator of overall investment returns.

- Funds can be tax efficient.

Funds can be tax efficient on a number of levels. I made a passing reference in an earlier chapter to funds that offer specific tax reliefs and tax advantages to the investor, but many of these require great care due to the risks to which they must be exposed in order to attract these tax advantages. Funds in general offer two potential tax advantages.

The first is that, although their income distributions are taxed, any capital gain on the sale of an underlying investment within the fund is tax-free. It is only when we sell our shares or units in the underlying fund itself that we might incur tax on the capital gain. However within an approved pension fund structure or an ISA there is neither income nor capital gains tax payable at any stage until a pension is drawn, so there is no specific *tax* advantage from investing through funds.

The second, and less obvious, advantage relates to fees. Outside a pension arrangement, a fee paid to a segregated fund manager (where a private individual's funds are looked after directly by a fund manager) is typically paid out of income which has already been taxed, whereas we receive the income distributed by many funds after fees and other administration costs have already been deducted, and income tax is only payable on the net amounts that we actually receive.

- Investors in funds have the protections provided by the fund managers' regulator.

  Although in my experience the financial regulators appear to focus on many issues that do not have any obvious relevance to the investors they are tasked to protect, there are occasions when they do provide investors with recourse for any adverse effects suffered from a fund manager's negligence without investors being forced into expensive litigation.

- Investors enjoy the protection of the fund managers' insurance

  A corollary of my previous point is that fund managers are forced by their regulators both to retain sufficient capital to enable them to operate safely and, as important, sufficient insurance to enable them to compensate investors when appropriate.

Fees

If you are lucky enough to be able to afford a fund manager or investment advisor, they will in most cases levy a fee based on the sums of money that they manage for you. Many private client fund managers also levy a dealing charge – typically a commission levied as a percentage according to the size of the trade, a compliance charge, which is a contribution towards their cost of regulation, and stamp duty – a government tax of 0.5% on share purchases.

If the fund manager then makes use of collective funds in order to gain exposures to specialist or overseas markets for the reasons described above, unless these funds' fees are offset against their management fees, the costs can account for a very significant proportion of the return. Add to this the fact that few managers regularly outperform the market indices, then these fees start to look onerous, and with relatively low inflation and commensurately low nominal percentage returns, fees can erode an even larger proportion of the return. Let me explain why.

In the high inflation era of the final 25 years of the last century, the percentage returns from cash, bonds and equities may have been volatile, but they were on the whole quite high. They may not have been high in *real,* inflation adjusted terms, but the annual percentage returns *were* high – often well into double digits. So if equities were growing and providing returns of, say, 20% each year, then the annual fee deducted by the fund managers of 1.5% were hardly noticeable.

Too much of our return disappears in fees

The situation is now very different. Despite the 2023 post Covid and Ukranian war inflation spike, the Bank of England's inflation target, let us assume a 'real', inflation-adjusted target annual return of 5% from your shares, means that we might have a total long-term return target of 7.5% (2.5% + 5%). If annual fees and charges remain at around 1.5% then they would remove up to 20% of our expected return, and a whopping 30% of the real return above inflation. Now let us assume that our manager invests some of our funds in an investment trust which charges another 1% in management fees and you are getting near to losing half of the expected return in fees, so the manager will have to generate outstanding performance to justify what he's getting paid. Many fund managers have now adjusted their fees to reflect these dynamics but this remains an important consideration when comparing managers and investment products. The higher the fee, the more risk must be taken on to achieve the same return and the more a manager must strive to mitigate costs through added performance.

Equity Income Funds

Here is a real life illustration of the problem – no names, no pack drill. Many private, long-term pension investors use a range of UK Equity Income funds, run by highly respected fund managers. These funds use a portfolio of high yielding shares to provide their investors with an income yield above that available from the stock market as a whole, and they try to grow both the value of the assets and the dividend income distributed to shareholders over time so that they at least match inflation. An attractive and useful objective you might agree. But here's the problem.

Firstly, as I explained in the share valuation chapter, those shares that offer the highest income today often do so because the markets do not expect them to be able to grow their profits and dividends as quickly as other companies in the future. You would therefore not expect these to be the fastest growing and best performing shares in the longer term. However I have no problem with this – we know that there's no such thing as a free lunch and that we may need to make some growth sacrifice if we seek a higher than average income immediately.

Now let's get back to the fees issue. Let us assume that we use these funds, as many do, as an immediate source of income, and use their dividends as income to pay the household bills. At the time of writing these funds are typically providing annual dividend income yields of around 4%. Now let's look at the underlying yield required to generate this.

We will assume the cost of running the fund – management fee, administrators, independent directors and compliance – amounts to 1.5%. So although the effects can be partially hidden by charging fees against the capital, the underlying assets must actually yield more than 4% to enable these dividends to be paid from the fund's income, and much more than the market as a whole that at the time of writing yields less than 4%. In other words, the management costs can remove over one third of the income that you would have received had you owned the underlying investments directly and not via a fund.

No honey, no money

'No problem,' I hear you say, if the managers are performing well and are providing something that we can't do ourselves. But if you have a moment, have a look at the publicly available online research that itemises the ten largest holdings of each of these UK Equity Income funds. Notice anything odd? They are quite similar. This is hardly surprising given that these funds are huge – some are several billions in value – and each has to choose from the same relatively small universe of large, safe shares that provide higher than average dividend income. My conclusion? Some feel that they have little choice but to accept this situation, but as a result they may need to save up to 30% more than if they had bought these investments directly and not via funds. Again, many managers have now decreased their fees but the issue remains.

It is therefore tempting to purchase some of these shares ourselves. Many are relatively safe and well diversified companies that you might want to hold forever and a day, but BP's appalling oil spill in the Gulf of Mexico and the subsequent costs of clearing it up and compensating those affected, provides a clear example of when an unexpected event can remove even a very large 'blue chip' company's ability to pay its dividend.

Watch out, too, for other seemingly safe high yielding sectors such as the utility companies, where political interference can constrain their operational and pricing freedom and affect their ability to grow their dividends to shareholders and more recently high levels of debt have increased the investment risk. If you want to cut the cost of a fund manager, informed advice and research will be required, even for the savviest private investor.

In summary, their fees are always worth paying if the manager either provides us with a return that regularly beats the relevant indices, or offers a spread of risk in a market where it is neither practical nor economic for us to invest directly into the underlying securities.

Open Ended vs Closed End Funds

We arrive finally at the difference between the two main types of fund to which I referred earlier – 'open' and 'closed' end.

Investment Trusts are public limited companies (PLC's) listed on the stock exchange and are closed ended. This means that investors buy and sell shares in these companies rather than require the managers to sell the underlying investments within the trust in order to redeem their investment.

Every day, the investment trust manager will announce the value of the underlying investments in the form of a Net Asset Value (NAV) attributable to each share. This is the value of the assets, less any liabilities, for example loans, divided by the total number of shares in issue. Although prices of investment trust shares are closely related to the NAV, seldom will the share price exactly mirror the NAV. Most investment trusts trade at discounts to NAV although some popular trusts do trade at premiums where the share price is actually greater than the value of the underlying assets.

An 'open ended' unit trust or investment company is, as the title suggests, an investment fund where a new investor buys new units or shares in the fund and the cash investment is sent to the manager to be invested. Conversely, a seller receives the sale proceeds via the sale of assets from the fund – unless of course there are sufficient new investors who wish to buy shares or units to match the sale requests, known as 'redemptions'. So when investors wish to buy and sell, units are created or cancelled.

So what are the advantages and disadvantages of these investment vehicles?

The advantages of closed end funds include:

- The ability to borrow (known as 'gearing' or 'leverage').

  If the underlying assets return more than the cost of the loans then the overall returns to the investors can be increased.

- No requirement to sell assets at inopportune times to meet redemptions.

  Sellers of investment trust shares need to find buyers for their shares and therefore the price they receive will be a function of supply and demand for their shares rather than solely the underlying value of the investments. The manager is therefore not forced to sell assets to satisfy investors who want to sell.

- The ability to buy illiquid assets, knowing that the manager will not be forced to sell to meet redemptions.

  This is a function of the previous point – some assets have insufficient liquidity to enable them to be managed in an open-ended fund where investors can only realize their investment when sufficient of the underlying assets can be sold, for example property, forestry assets or private equity.

- Investors can often buy investment trust shares at a discount to their underlying asset value.

  This of course works both ways, but when markets are depressed, discounts tend to be higher, so a successful contra cyclical investor can make money from two sources – the increase in the value of the underlying investments and the narrowing of the trust's share price discount to its NAV.

The main advantage of an open ended fund is that investors can buy and sell in the knowledge that they will, in normal circumstances, pay or receive the value of the underlying investments. However, those wishing to sell open-ended investments where the underlying assets are illiquid (expensive or difficult to sell quickly) may have to wait a considerable time for the proceeds, and if their requirement for liquidity is immediate they might receive a price considerably lower than the stated underlying asset value.

In the light of their advantages you could be forgiven for wondering why not *all* funds are closed ended. The short answer is that investment managers need to start with very significant sums of money for management within the fund to justify launching an investment trust and to cover the ongoing running costs of a publicly listed company. An open-ended fund can build up gradually and can start at a relatively small size. The cost of 'abort fees' to the sponsor of an unsuccessful investment trust launch can be very large and so the risk is significant.

The other main reason is in this age of investor's focus on short-term returns; new investment trusts have another related problem. Investment trust launches are costly – corporate finance advisers and lawyers charge significant sums, both to produce the legal paperwork which must comply with the stock exchange listing requirements, and to find investors for the fund. Stockbrokers will charge fees and commissions for placing the shares with investors and raising the money lawyers charge to produce the necessary documentation. So the investment trust's starting Net Asset Value will therefore be below the price paid by the investors, who will therefore fear that, unless the underlying assets rise quickly in value, their shares will show an initial loss, even if the shares do not trade at a discount to their asset value.

15

A Guide to Managing
Your Own Investments

"Tis the part of a wise man to keep himself today for tomorrow,
and not venture all his eggs in one basket."

– Miguel de Cervantes, Don Quixote de la Mancha, 1605.

"Behold, the fool saith, 'Put not all thine eggs in the one basket'
– which is but a manner of saying, 'Scatter your money and
attention;' but the wise man saith 'Put all your eggs in the one
basket and – WATCH that basket."

– Mark Twain, Pudd'nhead Wilson, 1894.

Cervantes and Twain were both great writers, but Cervantes would have made a better investor. In fact, diversification has been a key component of asset allocation for some time. A prominent magazine in 1926 recommended that a portfolio contain 25% sound bonds, 25% sound preferreds, 25% sound common stocks, and 25% speculative securities. This may not be an entirely appropriate portfolio distribution today, but the importance of asset allocation remains.

Now let's get back to what our savings are there to achieve. What is the final objective and how long can the investments remain in situ? Whatever the answer we must also to decide whether we might need access to some or even all of our savings at shorter notice if there is an unexpected crisis, or even an unexpected opportunity to invest in something particularly attractive. Of course the former reason does not apply to an approved pension plan because the money is locked in until you retire – and a very good thing too.

Investments for the long-term saver

Let's start with an illustration of a long-term pension saver with several decades to go until he or she reaches retirement age, and we will then consider how the investment strategy might change over that period to reflect a shortening time frame. The latter analysis might be of particular interest to readers who are themselves nearing retirement.

The analysis will be 'top down'. This term refers to the most important discipline of constructing a portfolio on the basis of which asset categories are most appropriate, before selecting any of the individual underlying investments. 'Bottom up' is not a form of encouragement to imbibe alcohol, it is the description of an approach used by some investors who prefer to ignore the allocation between asset categories and just select their preferred individual investments.

We now need to refer back to our earlier analysis of risk to decide how much of each risk category is appropriate in our quest for higher returns. So as we concluded then, an investor with a forty-year time horizon can, to all intents and purposes, ignore both volatility and liquidity risk and focus on investment risk – the risk that the investments may not provide the returns required to achieve the objective. In this case we relate investment risk to the objective of generating sufficient pension income to fund a decent lifestyle in forty years' time.

Now we need to look at the various asset categories and decide which are the most likely to provide 'real' returns above price inflation. In normal circumstances we agreed that the best match for a 'real' liability was some form of asset whose returns are likely to reflect, and hopefully exceed, the long-term increase in retail prices. This means that we should consider assets such as shares and property that I discussed earlier, because over extended periods their returns have reflected the changing value of money, a value that is eroded by rising prices. So can we agree that at the outset we should have the majority of our investments in this type of asset?

Now let's run through all of the alternative asset categories:

Cash and Bonds

Long-Term Returns Suggest 100% in Equities!

Between 1900 and 2011:

- £1 Invested in Equities è £16,394
- £1 Invested in Gilts è £315
- £1 Invested in Cash è £202

Source Barclays Equity Gilt Study 2012

So why should we consider holding *any* monetary assets such as cash and bonds when we have agreed that real assets are the best match for our liability?

Monetary assets can provide insurance, even for long-term investors

We need to accept that, on occasions, there can be benefits from separating long-term strategy from shorter-term tactics. Another more flippant description is that we should not always allow our long-term strategy to get in the way of a good short-term opportunity, and we can often be rewarded by departing from some of our core strategic investments that are the best match for our long term objectives in pursuit of attractive investment opportunities elsewhere.

Here are a few specific instances:

- There have been extended periods when monetary assets have performed very much better than share and property markets – particularly after financial shocks

- Monetary assets will perform better than real assets during periods of deflation when the prices of goods are falling and the value of our money is actually increasing

- We may not want to keep all of our eggs in the one asset basket

- The returns from monetary assets are sometimes not closely correlated to shares and can therefore remove some of our portfolio's overall volatility

- Even though cash and bonds currently provide returns below inflation, there have been periods when monetary assets have provided returns above inflation.

- Low risk monetary assets are typically both liquid and stable.

- A proportion of our funds might need to be kept liquid in case of unexpected expenses or other investment opportunities – for example if markets fall after an economic shock

So it can be advisable to diversify, even if this means investing some of our savings in assets that are not necessarily the most obvious match for our long-term liabilities, and doing so can, in some circumstances, actually increase our return while at the same time decreasing risk.

So how should we go about investing in monetary assets such as cash and bonds? Unless you fancy an exposure to high yielding – and therefore higher risk – corporate bonds, up until 2021 interest rates since the financial crisis in 2008 remained at such low levels that too much of our expected return from cash and Gilts could disappear in management fees if we were to invest through funds. So this is an area where, if the yields look attractive, we might want to consider investing directly into Gilts. At the time of writing cash and Gilts yield in excess of 4%.

Cash is quite simple: if we leave money immediately accessible in our current accounts we might receive some interest, but if we are prepared to lock into fixed term deposits then we are likely to be offered much more. However even if we can break that deposit before the end of the lock-in period, we could lose a significant proportion if not all of the interest, and so we need to ensure that we can do without our money until the end of the fixed deposit period.

The amount of cash that we should hold in a long term investment portfolio is dependent upon our confidence that it is sufficient to cover our foreseeable need for liquidity, but it can also be a function of the immediate availability of attractive long-term investments – although I will come back later to the dangers of trying to time our entry to the markets. Within my pension fund I hold as little cash as possible but I will usually retain between 3% and 5% of my investment portfolio in cash so that I am not forced to sell anything at short notice if an attractive buying opportunity presents itself.

As I explained earlier, the safest way to own bonds is through Gilt Edged Securities – bonds issued by the government. If we are prepared to take a little more risk and buy bonds issued by other borrowers such as companies, then we can generate a higher yield, but it is important to have access to advice and research on the companies that issue bonds so that we can understand the level of credit risk. This does not necessarily require the employment of an advisor or manager at great expense because many stockbrokers will provide research and offer their clients access to their advice in exchange for the commissions they earn when we decide to buy or sell securities. Some will also provide custody and administration services and even tax computations for a nominal fee, in exchange for the commissions that they earn from our trades.

So what proportion of their savings should a long term investor retain in bonds? The answer, I believe, is anything between nothing and not much, unless and until bonds can provide a return that matches or exceeds price inflation. By the time you read this, bond markets may have reached this level of yield, but at the time of writing their returns are still some way short of this benchmark, although they are closer than they were in late 2012 when there were fewer signs of economic recovery and long term interest rates were even lower. At the time of writing rates have risen form almost zero to over 5% – a little above inflation.

Equities

If we are feeling brave enough to invest at least a proportion of our savings directly into shares as opposed to via funds, how do we begin to construct a share portfolio?

Again we come back to the need for the diversification of risk. We do not want all of our eggs in one basket so we *must* have a spread of individual investments. So let's look at how the Stock Exchange is split up, and we'll start with the different merits of large and small companies.

Large listed companies have many advantages for private investors:

- Large company shares are liquid – easy and cheap to buy and sell

- Large companies are typically diverse with many having exposures across different businesses in a variety of industrial sectors.

- Many large companies offer investors international diversification

- All large companies announce regular trading updates to keep their investors informed

- Large companies are well researched and commentaries are widely available online and in accessible in publications such as newspapers

So why do we bother with small companies if they are riskier?

The answer is that historically small companies have grown more quickly than mature big ones, and investor returns have therefore been significantly higher. So how do we find the good, fast growing small companies that are not so well researched? The short answer is that we probably don't – this is where we are fully justified in investing through collective funds, the cost of which should be outweighed by the additional returns they generate from the small, faster growing companies in which they invest. Besides it is a more onerous task researching smaller companies because there are lots of them and there is less publicly available information, so we shouldn't begrudge good smaller companies fund managers their fees.

Diversification

So let's assume that we confine our direct investments to the very largest companies, defined as members of the FTSE 100 Share Index (FTSE). These are the one hundred largest companies listed on the London Stock Exchange, even though there are some within the mining and resources sectors in particular, which have their entire business outside the UK. So which to choose, and how do we ensure we have a spread? Let's start with sectors.

The FTSE is broken down into industry sectors, and so to achieve a spread of risk it must make sense to first ensure that we do not have too many shares in any one industrial sector. Different industries have different dynamics. They sell different goods and services to different customers in different places, so we should not concentrate our equity exposure in too narrow a segment of the economy:

FTSE 100 Index ICB Industry Breakdowns 31st December 2023

ICB Industry	Number of Companies	Index weighting
Energy	2	12.82%
Basic materials	7	9.42%
Industrials	19	13.18%
Consumer Staples	11	17.09%
Health Care	9	12.19%
Consumer Discretionary	24	7.17%
Communications	6	2.79%
Utilities	5	4.80%
Financials	20	19.07%
IT	21	1.07%

As we can see from the table above, nearly a fifth of the FTSE 100 Index, both by value and number of companies is made up of 'Financials' such as banks, insurance and property companies. This has not always been the case because the index is not static – companies outside the index whose market valuations grow can replace the smallest companies in the index that then fall out of the top one hundred. For example since June 2011 Energy has fallen from over 17% to under 13%, Communications (formerly Telecoms) has halved from a little under 6%, while Industrials has risen from 7.57% to 13.18% and Healthcare from 7.27% to 12.19%.

Most of the ICB sectors are self-explanatory but some do need breaking down into their sub-sectors:

- 'Basic Materials' include chemicals and other basic resources such as forestry & paper, metals and mining

- 'Industrials' breaks down into range of sub-sectors including construction & materials, aerospace and defence, engineering, electronic equipment, transport and support services

- 'Consumer Goods' include automotives & automotive parts, food & beverages, household goods, leisure goods and tobacco

- 'Consumer Services' represents retailers, media, travel and leisure

If we want a perfect spread that exactly matches the market index, we can opt to buy the entire index, i.e. every share in the FTSE 100, in the exact proportions that they represent in the index itself. The way to do this in a cost effective manner is to buy units in an index fund – a fund that replicates the index's return. This is known as 'passive' investing, and fees tend to be lower than those levied by 'active' managers who try to choose the best shares and provide returns above the index.

If you *are* attracted by the idea of investing at least some of your equity portfolio directly, again I would urge you to ensure that you have access to research and take professional advice. But how much money do we need before we can consider the option of investing direct? The short answer is that you must have sufficient to be able to achieve an adequate spread of investment risk at a reasonable cost.

The statistics module in my pre-historic economics degree taught me to assume that using normal distribution theory (defined in *The Glossary of Terms*), to achieve sufficient diversification we should have approximately thirty individual investments in total.

So if your directly invested share portfolio accounts for around two thirds of your total pension savings, then let's use twenty shareholdings as our target assumption – unless of course you have already diversified through funds, in which case you can justify buying fewer individual holdings.

How much do I need if I want to invest directly into shares, not funds?

So what's the minimum amount that we should invest in an individual share? This depends upon your stockbroker's commission rates, and in particular their minimum commission per contract.

There's limited science behind this conclusion, but let us say:

- That we don't want to pay commissions of more than 2.5% of the total amount invested in each share, and

- your broker's minimum commission per transaction is £50,then this would suggest that each individual investment should be of **at least** £2,000 in value,

- and twenty of these investments suggests that £40,000 is the very least that you should have available to invest in individual shares rather than exclusively through funds.

Many fund managers insist on several times this figure before they will invest directly in shares rather than via funds, but this might have more to do with their logistics, cost and profitability than necessarily their clients' interests. Given the cost of administration and collecting dividends I would suggest minimum units of £5,000 which implies an absolute minimum of £100,000 is required if we want 20 holdings or more – including some collective funds.

Many private investors opt for a 'core and satellite' strategy that entails holding a core of funds – actively managed or passive index funds – with some satellite holdings in some individual shares. This achieves the necessary spread of investments while allowing them to save fees and increase their income through some direct investments in a range of 'blue chip' shares. Bear in mind that even the index of the largest shares is itself highly concentrated in just ten giant companies:

FTSE 100 Index Portfolio Characteristics 31st January 2024

Total Valuation of Index Companies	£1,912 billion
Average Value of the Companies	£19 billion
Largest Company	£162 billion
Smallest Company	£1 billion
Largest Company as % of the Index	8.5%
Largest 10 Companies as % of the index	46%

Property

As I mentioned earlier, I would suggest that only the very largest private investors should consider investing directly into individual buildings – with one possible exception. Many self-employed savers into personal pensions make use of the option to purchase their own workplace – typically their offices – and pay rent into their own pension funds for their right to occupy. That aside I would strongly recommend achieving diversity through funds or shares. Property shares are represented within the FTSE 100 Index and so your twenty shares could include some property exposure.

Although there was talk under the previous Labour Chancellor Mr. Brown's tenure at the Treasury that residential property – and even a holiday home – was to be introduced as an approved pension asset, they changed their minds at the eleventh hour. Outside pensions of course there are many who have built successful leveraged 'buy to let' residential property portfolios, but you don't need me to expound the virtues and itemise the considerable risks involved and this and the changes which take away the ability to offset interest from loans against rental income. Moreover if you already own your own home then how many eggs do really want in the residential property investment basket?

Asset Allocation Parameters

There is no right or wrong way to build an investment portfolio but there must be a conscious and informed balance between the pursuit of the rewards that can be gained from exposing your savings to risk, and the necessity to mitigate these risks through diversity across a broad spread of investments. So here are some parameters that I have used for my own long-term pension savings:

- **Cash and Bonds:** 5%–15%, directly invested

- **UK and overseas equities:** 55%–75%, part directly invested, smaller companies and specialist sector and overseas exposures investment via collective funds

- **Property:** 5%–10%, all via property shares or funds

- **Alternatives, commodities and private equity:** 5%–15%, all in funds

I should add that many wealth management companies have a range of recommended allocations according to the 'risk appetite' of their clients. Here is a current example taken from the website of a respected US manager:

	Fixed Income (Bonds)	Equities
Conservative Allocation	70%	30%
Moderate allocation	60%	40%
Growth Allocation	25%	75%
Aggressive allocation	10%	90%

You will probably come across variations of this schedule, but in my view they can be dangerous over-simplifications and most probably indicate the advisor's fear of the financial industry regulators that focus their attention almost exclusively upon the risk of loss. I have already covered this issue in an earlier chapter, but this approach ignores the essential requirement to focus on our individual circumstances and objectives and set our strategic asset allocation parameters accordingly, and not some arbitrary and spurious notion of our personal appetite for volatility risk or the risk of short-term paper losses.

The Dangers of Market Timing

Finally we come to the timing of our share purchases. Ibbotson associates the American investment research and advisory firm to which I referred in an earlier chapter did some fascinating research in the 1980's that exposed the potential dangers of market timing. The term 'market timing' describes an investment approach that attempts to time purchases and sales of equities in order to enjoy 'Bull Markets' – extended periods when markets rise – and avoid 'Bear Markets'

when markets fall. Sounds a great idea but in practice this approach is fraught with danger to the long-term investor.

Ibbotson demonstrated that long-term share market returns had been concentrated into relatively short periods when markets can rise very dramatically, and over the 70 year period that they studied, if an investor had missed just the thirty best months' returns from US shares, then virtually all of the relative benefits of equity investment vs. monetary assets would have been lost.

Nobody rings a bell when the markets are about to fall or rise, and there is an old adage that the night is seldom darker than just before dawn. This danger is a truism – something that confirms what we already know to be fact. Without wishing to labour the point, markets reach highs because everything looks rosy and reach lows because all looks lost, so few investors manage in practice to be sufficiently brave to invest when all others are in despair, or sell while the party is still in full swing.

There are, however, measures of value which can provide useful yardsticks, and on occasion we might try to be at the conservative end of our asset allocation parameters as listed above if valuations appear stretched, and at the higher end of our equity range when share valuations look historically cheap.

But we should never depart entirely from asset categories that we think offer the best chance of meeting our long-term objectives. We might consider owning more defensive low beta shares when economic conditions look grim. Utility companies, food retailers and other less cyclical businesses tend to fare better than those exposed to commodities or manufacturing during recessions, but it is often difficult to be brave enough to switch back into more volatile growth shares in time for the upturn. Over the mid 1970's secondary banking crisis and a total equity meltdown, the best performance came from the bank that did absolutely nothing and rode the storm. Lazards.

Valuing Shares and Equity Markets

I have already covered measures of equity value in individual companies ,and the two main variables that are often used as yardsticks to compare valuations to historical 'norms' – dividend yields and Price: Earnings (PE) ratios. The Market's valuation merely extrapolates these measurements to include the aggregated valuations of an investment in every share in that index.

The overall market's dividend yield and PE ratio are indications of its current valuation but these measures should not be looked at in isolation. Let's go back to the Yield Gap analysis that related the dividend yields from shares to the interest rates available from Gilts.

If the interest rates available on cash and bonds rise, we might expect investors to demand higher returns from more risky assets in order to maintain their *relative* valuations, and vice versa. This is why we need to be particularly wary of asset price bubbles which have pushed equity and property valuations above historical norms, particularly in the residential housing market, because when interest rates remain low for extended periods, house buyers can borrow cheaply to buy property, investors can't get much if any return from cash and so search more aggressively for better returns elsewhere.This can cause demand for riskier assets to outstrip supply and as a result prices rise and if stretched too far valuations can come under threat when interest rates rise. This I referred to earlier the case of the Nasdaq Index which rose very dramatically eye-watering valuations in 2020 and 2021 before collapsing 40% in less than a year as rates started to rise.

So what if the value of our shares falls?

Before I leave the subject of timing and the market's valuation, I want to touch on one of my hobbyhorses – a concept that seems to have been lost in the stampede of bright young things intent on making investment analysis appear more complicated. The Dividend Discount Model is a method of valuing a company on the basis that its shares are worth the discounted sum of all its future dividend payments. It sounds fearsomely dull, but it is an important concept for us to understand.

Here's why:

Once we have bought our portfolio of investments, even though we may have convinced ourselves of the merits of a long-term acceptance of volatility risk, we would not be human if we did not want to check the value of our investments on a regular basis. Quite right too if we are to keep up with their progress and make occasional changes where necessary. But should we not worry if the value of our shares falls?

As I mentioned earlier, volatility and liquidity risk are less relevant for a long-term investor. Markets will inevitably have their short-term wobbles, but these will typically resemble small bumps along the long-term share price chart. We should only worry if the underlying assumptions that we made at the time we invested no longer hold true. At an individual company level there will be times when we conclude we have made a mistake and we should sell an investment and find a better one.

But if the fundamental value remains, just because the market decides to place a lower value on the shares in the short term, it does not necessarily imply that their intrinsic worth is less than the amount that we paid at the time we made the original investment.

The same goes for the markets themselves. After the 1987 'Black Monday' (and Tuesday) stock market crash, what had actually changed? Not a lot, as it turned out, and market index soon recovered. Yes, the markets did look a bit stretched, but it was the hedge fund program traders' computer-driven investment strategies that set the falls in motion in Hong Kong, and the crash rippled across the world as stock markets in each time zone opened and reflected the panic whipped up by those markets that were closing at the end of their day's trading. What a buying opportunity it turned out to be!

In days gone by, when God was in short trousers and I was starting out as a wet-behind-the-ears fund manager, the consulting actuaries that advised the big company pension funds looked at falls in market values much more pragmatically. If the underlying earnings and income from the investments in the fund remained unchanged, then they sensibly concluded that the actuarial value of the pension fund had not changed either.

We should not worry too much that the market value of an investment has fallen. If the underlying fundamental values and assumptions that we considered attractive when we bought the shares remain intact, then whatever the share price, nothing has changed, truth will out in the end and the share price will recover in time.

In other words, if you get the earnings assumptions right over the long-term, then the capital values will look after themselves.

Shortening investment time horizons

Now let's consider the saver with an initial forty year investment horizon, thirty years on. There's ten years to go until he or she intends to retire and will need to extract an income from these investments, so should the asset allocation parameters be altered? Ten years is still a healthy amount of time for equity investment but it is certainly time to be considering the appropriate balance of our investments as we get nearer to our chosen retirement age. So what sort of changes might we consider and when should we start the move towards this new allocation?

Let's start with conventional wisdom and then show why this might now be inappropriate and even dangerous. It is absolutely crucial that we understand the amount of risk that most of us will now need to take with our pension assets, even *after* we retire, and although following the changes in the 2014 Budget we are no longer forced to buy annuities to provide income for retirement, many may still be advised to do so. This is another example of the backside covering that is forced onto financial advisors by their one-dimensional regulators and can prevent them from offering appropriate advice.

Lifetime Annuities

"If we take a late retirement and an early death, we'll just squeak by."

First let me explain annuities to those who haven't yet come across them. An annuity is the product of an informed bet that an insurance company provider takes on how long we will live. In its simplest form we hand over a lump sum of money and they will pay us an agreed level of income for as long as we remain alive. If we pop our clogs after a couple of years then they win and take all the cash. But if we defy the statistical probabilities and live longer than their mortality tables suggest, then we win and receive this income for longer than the annuity provider had expected. So if you want to get the best annuity rate quotations from your insurance company, keep smoking, keep drinking and remain overweight!

The annuity's rate of return will reflect a return of our capital over our expected lifetime, plus the returns from the Gilts into which our money is invested, minus of course a profit margin for the insurance company. Because life insurance companies sell lots of annuities, the longer livers are offset by the early leavers. Sounds fine doesn't it? No risk and a higher return than Gilts, some of which can be tax-free because it is a notional return of our own capital.

So where is the catch? The problem is that these products were originally designed when interest rates were much higher and average life expectancies were far shorter than they are now. Long-term interest rates had already been falling for some years but they collapsed further after the financial crash in 2008. So up until 2022 it appeared that we would need to save much more in order to buy the same amount of annuity income. Rates have now risen and so until inflation returns to the Bank's target and they fall back, maybe annuities will offer better value to elderly buyers. However the other catch is that if we are now expecting to live for several decades in retirement, this both lowers the annual amounts we receive from annuities and also requires some insurance against price inflation. Because of this, income from inflation-indexed annuities can be lower.

In conclusion, annuities are preferably bought later in life when the returns are higher, because the older we are, the shorter time the mortality tables suggest we are likely to live and the more the annual income the insurance company is prepared to pay out. So how do we extract an income from our savings after retirement for the rest of our lives, and how might we want to restructure our investments over the decade before we retire?

So how can we take a 5% annual income from our savings?

Back to conventional wisdom, or in this case, outdated thinking. When annuities were the answer, then as savers approached retirement, their funds would be moved gradually away from the volatility of shares and other real assets, towards the assets that best matched their liability – in this case the purchase of an annuity. So what was the best match? Because annuity rates are a function of age, life expectancy and long-term interest rates, the obvious match was a long-dated government bond and so during the years leading up to retirement their funds would be moved gradually into Gilts.

As we approach retirement we need to seek individual advice because our circumstances and priorities will be particular to us and so there is therefore no one solution that fits us all, but here are some basic principles that I hope you will provide useful sense-checks with which to challenge any advice you are offered, and particularly if you are ever advised to buy an annuity.

So let's now revert to the amount of income that we can take from our pensions and other savings to pay the bills when we stop earning, and cast our minds back to the beginning to the savings discussion in Chapter 11, where we used an assumption of 5% per annum. You will remember that real assets provided the best match for 'real', inflation-adjusted incomes, and so to move wholesale into monetary assets as we approach retirement would appear counter-intuitive and illogical, because we *know* that cash and bonds have historically done rubbish job at protecting real incomes over the longer term. *And* we are living longer so the chances of the same fixed income being sufficient to keep us fed, watered and housed in thirty years' time are worse than slim.

Post retirement, asset allocation is just as important

One glimmer of light has appeared from a most surprising source – the same short-sighted politicians that got us into this mess in the first place. Defined Contribution pension savers may have been much abused over recent years but hallelujah, we are now no longer forced by the pension rules to buy annuities and we can therefore remain invested in real assets even after we retire.

So if we've saved enough, we can probably survive in reasonable comfort if we structure our savings sensibly both within and outside our approved pension arrangements, and this is in large part because we are now able to retain our shares, property and other investments within our pension funds until we die and beyond if the kids don't cash in!. We can therefore continue to invest in a manner that, while not guaranteed, is more likely to provide returns that will allow us to extract our inflation adjusted 5% as an income for the remainder of our lives.

Should we not de-risk investments before retirement?

That is not to say that we shouldn't consider any adjustment to our asset allocation as we get closer to retirement. We may wish to de-risk our pension funds and other savings and invest in less volatile, safer shares that offer relatively high and sustainable yields, and exchange lower growth prospects for higher income and less volatility. For example the utility companies and infrastructure funds often communicate their income growth targets – usually announced as inflation plus a percentage, and many of these shares at the time of writing provided dividend income yields of around 6%. Alternatively we can retain more of our high growth shares and balance the need for less volatility and more income by increasing our bond holdings, depending on market conditions and the yields available at the time.

If we can survive on the returns that our savings provide until we are much older, then we can start to draw on our capital – perhaps to pay for more expensive care as we get older, and we can even use the equity in our homes to supplement our incomes through equity release or downsizing if required. And if we survive long enough then who knows, it may even be sensible to bet on a very long life and use part of our pension assets to buy an annuity.

It would all be so much easier if someone could tell us how long we are going to live, then we could plan our finances more accurately and ensure that we spend all of our kids' inheritance before we die, but we don't, so that's why I felt the need to write this book!

Do I have to live just off my investment income?

One more thing before I move on to my final bête noire. People often ask whether they should only spend the income generated from their investments, or whether it's OK to spend some of the capital itself. As I suggested in the introduction to this book, it is of course much easier to spend than to accumulate capital, but this is a completely different point.

There are two main factors to consider. First we need to consider the optimum balance between the generation of income or capital gain from our investments. Returning to our assumed core of investments in real assets (as opposed to monetary assets), we assume that in normal circumstances we might need to accept a lower initial income by investing in the shares of companies whose dividends we expect to grow over time, whereas fixed income bonds, as their name suggests, offer a fixed rate of return until they are repaid. I have already alluded to the fact that although we currently have a yield gap and many shares yield more than cash or bonds, in the inflationary environment that we expect to return to when economies pick up I would be surprised if this were to continue indefinitely.

Let's now go back to our 5% income assumption. Does every investment need to provide income of at least 5%? No, of course not. Some of our high growth investments or private equity funds may not provide much if any income at all. So if we are to extract 5% each year from our investments it is likely to be from a combination of income and gains in the value of our investments. Remember that the reason we often accept lower initial dividend income from some shares is that the company's earnings and dividends are expected to grow over time – and by the time we retire the yield on our original purchase cost could be very substantially higher.

Don't allow the income tail wag the investment dog, but hold more cash

We should not allow the choice between the generation of capital gain or income to dominate our investment strategy. Our only constraint should be our level of acceptable risk. Our objective *must* be to invest our savings in a manner designed to fill the savings pot as full as possible, but within our personal appetites for risk, and we should not mind too much whether the return arrives in the form of income or capital gain.

One caveat however. Once our income is sitting in our bank account it is ours and nobody can take it away. If we wait to realise a capital gain, until the investment is actually sold, this gain only exists on paper and is therefore at risk from a change in market sentiment, or the outlook for the specific investment itself. It therefore provides some comfort to have a significant proportion of our income generated from investment income, and to avoid selling into weak market conditions we might want to hold higher amounts of cash once we start withdrawing an income from our savings.

Income from Pensions

Prior to the 2014 Budget there were strict rules that governed how much we could draw down from our pensions each year. These rules have now been relaxed, but all the income that we draw from our pension investments is still treated, and taxed, as income, whether the cash extracted from the pension fund was generated from income or capital.

The rules that govern the rate at which we can draw income from our pensions assumed that as we get older we need to draw down some of the capital, and the former pension's income 'Cap' on drawdowns rose as a percentage of our pension fund's value as we got older. These rules have been relaxed and it is now up to us to ensure that our savings can provide us with an income for as long as we live, but even if our pension fund and other savings perform well, our investments may not grow fast enough to prevent the need for some erosion of the capital. Besides, what is left in our pension funds when we die used to be taxed at an even higher rate than the Inheritance Tax payable on the rest of our estate. Anyway, I promised not to embark on a pension's tutorial so we'll move swiftly on.

Tax issues

The second issue relates to tax. Within our pensions and ISA's, the capital gain that we enjoy when the value of our investments rises remains free of tax, and it is only distributions from our pension funds that are taxed as income. I therefore need to remind you again to dust off the ISA rulebook, which confirms that neither gains nor income are taxable, whether it is reinvested or taken out of the ISA as income. This is a particularly valuable advantage. Remember that when we crystalise our pensions and start to draw an income we can take 25% of the value of our pensions as a tax-free lump sum and manage these funds with far greater flexibility, outside our pensions arrangements. your combined income as tax-efficiently as possible between you and your partner or spouse – or even your adult children. Everyone above the age of eighteen has an untaxed income allowance, so if one of you is not taking full advantage of this, then perhaps you could consider moving the ownership of some income-producing assets to the members of your household who will pay the lowest amount of tax on the income.

16

Taxation

Taxation is another element of economics where a basic understanding can be useful. The government collects taxes from a variety of sources to provide the money to spend on our behalf, and taxation can alter people's behaviour – spending, saving and even their appetite for work or to remain in the UK.

Changes in taxes or tax rates can also have significant effects on the returns we receive from our investments, both because of how they affect the proportion of our investment income that we retain for our own use rather than pay out in tax, and the way in which they can affect taxpayer's behaviour. In the same way, companies' behaviour can be altered by changes in the taxation of their profits, and so for all of these reasons investors should have at least a basic knowledge and understanding of our tax system.

It is not my intention (or ability!) to arm readers with a comprehensive tax manual, so I have tried to limit my explanations to those major taxes that can alter the economic behaviour of those who pay them.

There are two basic categories of taxation – direct and indirect. Direct taxes, such as income tax, are levied directly from us and in most cases if we are employed (as opposed to self-employed) the tax has already been subtracted from our earned income before it arrives in our bank accounts. Indirect taxes such as VAT and excise duties are collected when we spend our money, and with the exception of food, children's clothing, magazines and newspapers, a significant proportion of everything we spend is handed over in VAT (currently 20%) or exise taxes on petrol, booze and ciggies to the Inland Revenue, the Government's tax collection arm.

So these are the main sources of UK taxation together with some ideas as to how these taxes might alter behaviour in a manner that could affect the economy and, as a result, alter the expected returns from our investments. In some cases I have indicated the current levels of tax but please be aware that rates of taxation change regularly and so by the time that you read this chapter they may already be out of date. Current tax rates are available on the HMRC website.

Income Tax

Income tax when taken directly from our salaries and levied through a system called PAYE (Pay As You Earn), apart from

170

some self-employed who can set aside the required amounts for a single annual payment. Income tax rates rise in bands – everyone has a 'nil rate' personal allowance which is an amount of income that an individual (or couple if only one is earning) can receive each year before any tax is paid. The tax year runs from the 6th April until the 5th April the following calendar year and at the time of writing the Income Tax bands rise thereafter from 20% to a top rate of 45%. This tax is assessed on all income, whether earned as salary or 'unearned' income from our investments. Note that the' nil rate' band currently erodes as incomes rise above £100,000 p.a. resulting in an effective 60% income tax band between £100,000 and £125,000.

Changes in income tax rates and tax bands can affect our behaviour in a number of ways. As I alluded to in my short description of Keynesian economics, increases in taxation can be used for the specific purpose of reigning in consumer spending when economic growth and inflation threaten to rise too fast. Conversely, during recessions when the economy needs a boost, taxes can be cut leaving more money in our pockets to spend and the government borrows to make up the shortfall in tax revenue.

In terms of our personal behaviour, if income taxes rise and we have less income available to spend, then perhaps the first areas of expenditure to be cut will be what we term 'discretionary' or non-essential spending. So when taxes rise we might want to review the outlook for companies exposed to these areas of spending such as holidays, the luxury ends of the food and restaurant industries, expensive cars or jewellery. In recent years some companies that service or supply these sectors have been insulated from squeezes on spending by the growing demand for luxury items from newly enriched people from the Middle East, Russia and China, but there is no question that the larger supermarket's loss of market share to discount food retailers such as Lidl and Aldi was directly related to a squeeze on household incomes after the 2008 financial crisis and the 2022/3 cost of living crisis – or whenever household incomes rise less quickly than prices.

Leaving these income tax bands unchanged during periods of high inflation was Chancellor Hunt's 'stealth tax', as a larger proportion of personal income is dragged into higher tax bands as wages rise. The term for this is 'fiscal drag'. So people's spending habits are affected by anything that changes the amount of income that they take home to spend or save.

And then there is the question of motivation. High levels of direct taxation can form a disincentive to hard work and ambition. When taxes have been at their highest, many people have reduced their work commitments to avoid paying higher tax rates, stopped work altogether or moved overseas to a more benign tax environment, rather than continue working hard for lower financial reward. I for one can honestly say that my decision to retire in my early 50's was partly linked to this disincentive. An effective marginal tax rate of over 60% on the first £1 that my wife and I earn over £100,000, together with 20% VAT and ever increasing excise duties on fuel, drink and tobacco had returned total taxation to well over 80p of every £1 that I earned, so I'd rather stay at home, earn less, write books and rely on my tax free ISA income to plug the gap!

So from a purely economic perspective, the optimum rates and bands of income tax are those that over the long-term raise the maximum amounts of tax revenue while creating the fewest distortions in the behaviour of taxpayers. It has been proven on occasion that falls in rates of direct taxation can actually *increase* the overall tax revenue as people work harder and spend less on expensive accountants to help mitigate tax, but as we all know, income tax rates are sometimes adjusted according to politically rather than economically motivated agendas.

National Insurance (NI)

National Insurance Contributions (NIC) operate like income tax and where possible are also removed directly from our pay packets through PAYE. The reason this form of taxation is referred to as insurance is because it is specifically designed to build our entitlements to certain state benefits, such as our old age state pensions or our rights to certain unemployment benefits if we find ourselves out of work. My inbuilt cynicism leads me to suspect that its separation from income tax gives an illusion of lower tax rates, particularly as our NIC contributions are not kept separate for the claimed purposes and are just added to the general taxation pot. Note that people of State Pension age cease to pay NIC on their earnings and so recent falls in NIC have only benefitted workers below this age – whereas a fall in income tax would have benefitted everyone.

NIC is paid both by employers who pay NIC on their payrolls and employees who pay the full rate only on a band of earnings and at a reduced rate thereafter. As such, changes in the rate of employers NIC have a direct effect on the cost of employing people, and any increase is an additional drain on a company's earnings and can therefore act as a disincentive to retain or hire employees. At the time of writing, NIC adds up to a significant addition to the cost of employing someone – a significant additional expense, but a fraction of that paid in France and many European countries.

The problem with NIC lies in its title. Whether we like it or not, governments are legally empowered both to levy taxes and spend the tax revenues as they see fit. As taxpayers, our only recourse is to vote for a different party of government at the next election. Insurance is different because we believe that once we have bought insurance it becomes ours by right. The difficulty comes when governments try to change the value or the basic terms of what contributors have been funding throughout their working lives.

Imagine approaching the till at a supermarket to buy a loaf of bread and between the till and the shop's exit someone informs us that the bread we've purchased isn't ours and removes it from our trolley without compensation. A riot would ensue and we would expect the loaf be returned to its rightful owner.

Now relate this story to an increase in the age when we will start to receive our state pensions after decades of contributions. If pension provision had been non-contributory and had just been funded through central taxation, then the alteration of the benefit might still be unpalatable but perhaps less controversial, given that most of us now understand that longer lives mean that we should not expect the same amounts of money to enable pensions to be paid over longer periods. I apologise for this departure from aspects directly related to the core issues of taxation but I thought that you might find the analogy interesting.

Capital Gains Tax (CGT)

Capital Gains Tax is levied on the profits we generate when we sell assets that are not exempted from the tax such as our primary residence. Everyone over the age of 18 has an annual CGT allowance – rather like for Income Tax- which allows them to take profits up to this amount exempt from tax, and any losses from previous years can be added to this allowance before the tax becomes payable. The nil rate CGT allowance was halved to £6,000 in 2023/4 and halved again in 2024/5. In Labour's first budget in 2024 CGT was raised from 10% to 18% for basic rate taxpayers and from 20% to 24% for higher rate taxpayers.

CGT raises relatively little money and is expensive to collect, but its justification revolves around addressing the potential distortion of investor's behaviour that would be likely to occur if there was no tax levied on capital gains. If we only paid tax on the income generated by our investments, and not on the capital profits generated when we sell, strategies to minimise the payment of tax would probably be more focused on the generation of capital profits. The Zero Coupon Preference share market was specifically developed by me, among others, to provide a return that mirrored what we might expect from a low risk bond, but was treated as a capital gain for taxation purposes. To address this distortion and level the playing field between income and capital gains, taxes on the latter are a necessary evil, but I will outline later the strategies available to minimise exposure to this and other taxes.

VAT

VAT stands for Value Added Tax, and most of our knowledge of this tax is limited to the fact that it currently adds 20% to the cost of almost everything we buy. VAT is an indirect tax because we pay it only when we spend our money. Although possibly not realistic as a tax avoidance strategy, we could choose not to spend our income on VAT'able goods, thereby avoiding the tax altogether.

As the title would suggest, VAT is payable on each stage of the value adding process. So let's use a very simple example of the manufacture of a car:

- The manufacturer of a car's component buys the materials that they need for £1 and they pays 20% VAT and so their total cost of these materials is £1.20

- The component manufacturer makes the component and sells it to the car manufacturer for £2, adds 20% VAT, and receives a total of £2.40. So the component manufacturer has recouped the 20p VAT that they paid for the materials and has collected a further 20p on the value that they've added before selling the component to the car manufacturer.

- The car manufacturer then sells the final product to the end user for £3 which reflects the added value they have been generated by assembling the car. On this amount is added 20% VAT which means the car buyer pays £3.60. The car manufacturers have therefore recouped both the 40p in VAT that they paid to the component manufacturer and collected the additional 20% on their value added of £1, so the government has collected the full amount of VAT.

From an economic and investment perspective the importance of VAT is, as with many other forms of tax, its effect on consumer's spending. Higher indirect taxes also decrease our capacity to buy goods and services in a similar way to taxes that remove a proportion of our incomes. However the difference is that VAT is paid by everyone who lives or spends time in the UK. Income tax misses non taxpayers and the 'Black Economy', tourists and other temporary visitors who pay their taxes elsewhere, and so it captures fewer people and as a result the tax burden is less evenly spread.

So what are the other economic effects of indirect taxes such as VAT? Well firstly for a year following a change in the rate of VAT, up or down, there is a direct knock on effect on the rate of inflation because the prices of virtually all goods and services will be affected. A change in the rate of inflation can itself have many knock-on effects on the underlying economy as, for example, employees demand higher wages to compensate, which in turn could lead to alterations in Britain's price competitiveness in relation to its trading partners.

Excise Taxes

Excise taxes are similar to VAT in that they are indirect taxes levied, at very much higher rates, from products such as alcohol, cigarettes and fuel. These products have been seen as a soft touch by politicians because not only do they raise lots of money but they also allow the government to claim the high moral ground from increasing tax on undesirable goods that either make people ill or pollute the atmosphere.

From a stock market perspective, the share prices of companies whose products or services are affected by these taxes tend to react in the short-term to annual tax rises that are either higher or lower than expected.

Inheritance Tax (IHT)

When we die, a specific monetary amount from our estate – the total value of the assets that we owned at the time of death – can

be passed on free of any tax. If we are married or have a permanent partner, each can, if they so choose, leave the other any amount of value without incurring a tax liability. Each partner has their own individual allowance and so, on the second death, the beneficiaries of a will – those who they have been chosen to inherit – will benefit from twice the individual nil rate band and at the time of writing will pay 40% tax on the value of assets above this amount.

The relevance of this tax to the wider economy is less obvious and pronounced, but if your assets amount to a value that exceeds the untaxed allowance you might want to consider some possible strategies if you wish to minimise this potential tax burden on your beneficiaries:

- Transfer assets that you don't need during your lifetime, and if you survive for seven years after the gift is made, the value of the assets transferred will be outside of your estate and will therefore be excluded from the IHT computation. Such transfers are termed 'Potentially Exempt' because the full exemption is only received if you survive for seven years following the transfer and have no longer had use or benefit from these assets.

If you continue to benefit from the assets that you transfer – for example a second home that you still use on occasion – then the transfer is deemed to be a 'Gift with Reservation' and will *not* be outside of your estate and so will still form a part of the value used to calculate the IHT liability.

- Every year we each have an annual gift allowance that allows a set sum to be given away without the restrictions that are applied to Potentially Exempt Transfers

- Missing out a generation can also provide a useful strategy to minimise IHT. If all assets are passed down one generation at a time, then there is a danger that the same asset, when passed down to the second generation, will be taxed again. It is often neither possible nor desirable, but missing a generation can save tax. The payment of grandchildren's school fees is not seen as a gift with reservation because it is parents rather than grandparents who are deemed to benefit.

- Even if the decision to miss a generation was not taken before the time of death, the beneficiaries of a will have up to two years following to decide if they wish to forego some or all of their inheritance in favour of others, for example their children. This can be done quite easily and cheaply through a Deed of Variation.

- There are some assets that are suffer inheritance tax at a lower rate. These currently include EIS, agricultural land and property, forestry, VCT's, some AIM listed shares, but the nature and availability of these reliefs is complex and so specialist tax planning and advice are essential.

Corporation Tax

Corporation Tax is a tax payable by companies on their profits. The definition of profit is a complex beast, so for these purposes let's simplify the definition to total income from sales minus total costs, and a percentage of this profit is paid in tax. In many cases amounts invested back into the business can be offset against taxable profits and used to decrease the tax paid. However, the problem with collecting Corporation Tax is that many of the largest international companies have businesses and even their head offices anywhere in the world and so are able to arrange for their profits to be generated in the areas with the lowest rates of tax.

So, unlike VAT or income tax, Corporation Tax is to some extent a voluntary tax, and countries have begun to compete by using lower employment costs and corporate tax rates (and in some cases large subsidies), to attract businesses to their jurisdictions to provide employment and raise tax revenue. More recently, significant increases in the rate of UK Corporation tax have been to an extent offset by more generous investment allowances.

From a pure investment perspective, the lower the taxes levied on the companies into which we invest, the higher the earnings they have available to reinvest or distribute to us as dividends, but when companies have been seen to blatantly rearrange their affairs in order to avoid tax and it becomes obvious that profits are being generated a long way away from the sales that generate them, then both consumers and governments have been known to act – the former through negative publicity and a boycott of the products, the latter through invasive examinations of the companies' financial affairs to ensure that profits earned in their domestic economy are not being sheltered in a low tax haven.

The other investment-related effect of corporate taxation is a company's valuation ratios. For the purposes of calculating a company's earnings multiple (a key value measurement) analysts often use earnings after tax has been paid to achieve a true comparison of distributable earnings. The earnings multiple therefore reflects the rate of Corporation Tax paid and any changes in this rate will therefore change the earnings multiple.

Tax efficiency

In pure economic terms, any tax that alters people's behaviour is inefficient – if you believe in the free market principle that resources are most efficiently allocated according to the balance of supply and demand, because it distorts the market's pricing mechanism. However, some taxes are more inefficient than others, and a more efficient tax is defined as one which is cheap and easy to collect and raises the most revenue without significantly altering the behaviour of those that pay it. On this basis a purchase tax such as VAT might be considered more efficient than progressive taxes on income.

There are hundreds of additional taxes in the UK's complex tax system, ranging from taxes on new pub leases and higher stamp duty on more expensive house purchases, and share transactions, to car tax and taxes levied on air travel and insurance policies, each of which can distort spending behaviour. Some, such as stamp duty on house purchases can have far reaching long-term effects both on the values placed on properties and the mobility of labour, or in the case of a share transaction tax can incentivise investors to move their business out of the UK to a lower taxed location.

Taxes that cause dramatic changes in behaviour are by their very nature inefficient, and unless there is a beneficial or justifiable social or financial side effect they should not be levied. The most inexcusable taxes are those which raise little revenue but create disproportionate changes in behaviour, often imposed for political or ideological 'virtue signalling' reasons rather than on the basis of their economic or redistributive benefits.

Taxation of Investment

Finally we come to the effects of taxation on the returns that we receive from our investments, and I will start with the tax treatment some of the tax- efficient savings arrangements that are currently available starting with pensions which are covered in more detail in a later chapter:

Saving via Pensions

- Pension savings are tax free at the point of entry – contributions to pensions can be made out of gross, untaxed earned income

- There are limits on the total amounts that can be contributed to pensions in a single year

- Limits to annual contributions have fallen over recent years

- There used to be strict rules as to when and how much pensions can pay out in a single year, but although rules relating to the age when we can start drawing pensions remain, Mr Osborne's 2014 Budget relaxed restrictions over the amounts that can be drawn.

- At the time that all or part of a pension is crystallised with a view to starting to take benefits, 25% of the amount to be crystallised can be taken out of the pension tax free up to a capped maximum level.

- The income extracted from a pension suffers income tax

ISAs

- There is a maximum amount that can be invested in ISA's in an individual year
- ISA's can only be purchased by people over 18
- There is no tax on the income produced by investments within an ISA
- There is no tax on any capital gains made within an ISA
- Any income taken from an ISA is free of tax
- Income or capital can be taken out of an ISA and returned at any time in the same financial year without tax

Taxation of Dividends

I have covered the effects of changes in the way tax is raised on dividends in an earlier chapter, but for the purposes of this description I will confine my comments to the tax itself.

Advanced Corporation Tax (ACT) was a scheme under which UK companies made an advanced payment of tax when they paid dividends to shareholders. This payment meant that those who received the dividends were considered to have already paid basic rate income tax on their dividends. Investors who were not liable to income tax, such as pension funds and charities, could reclaim this tax and therefore received their income free of any taxation.

In 1993 this link between ACT and basic rate Income Tax was broken and in 1999 ACT was scrapped altogether but 10% tax relief on dividend income continued. In 1997 tax relief for pension funds was scrapped completely.

17

Glossary of Terms

- **ACT**: The Advance Corporation Tax scheme allowed companies to make an advanced payment of tax when they paid dividends to shareholders. This meant that shareholders were deemed to have already paid tax at the basic rate on the dividends that they received and only needed to pay higher rate tax if required. Untaxed investors such as pension funds could therefore reclaim the tax paid on their dividends. In 1997 this tax relief for non-taxpayers was scrapped completely.

- **AIM**: the Alternative Investment Market is a market upon which companies can list without having to abide by some of the more onerous reporting and disclosure rules that apply to companies quoted on the main stock exchange. Some AIM listed shares suffer lower rates of Inheritance Tax.

- **Alpha** is a measure of the additional return from a portfolio of assets that is attributable to the manager's success in selecting the best investments.

- **Annuity** is an annual income guaranteed and paid by an insurance company for the life of the annuity's owner, in exchange for a fixed, non-returnable, lump sum investment. The older the buyer the higher the income because that the period that income is paid is likely to be shorter.

- **Approved Pension** is an investment fund into which companies and individuals can invest without paying corporation or income tax respectively on their contributions.

- **Asset Allocation** is a term for the proportions in which money is invested between the various asset classes.

- **Asset Class** is a generic type of investment, for example cash, bonds, equities or property.

- **Baby Boomer:** someone born in the two decades following the Second World War when the birth-rate recovered very dramatically, causing a bulge in the population of this age group.

- **Base Rate** is the interest rate set by the Bank of England's Monetary Policy Committee for lending to other banks. The level of interest rates is an important ingredient in the monetary policy that is used to control inflation. If the economy is growing too quickly and causing inflation then interest rates will rise. Borrowing costs for companies and individuals will therefore increase and expenditure is likely slow down as a result. Conversely when the economy is in recession and shrinking, lower interest rates can incentivise people and companies to borrow to increase spending and investment.

- **Beta** is an investment risk measurement that analyses historic movements of an individual share relative to its index. A Beta of more than 1.00 means that the share has historically moved, up or down, more that the market. A Beta of less than 1.00 means that the share has been less volatile than the market as a whole.

- **Bitcoin** is the best known cryptocurrency.

- **Blockchain** technology is a shared ledger for recording transactions, tracking assets and building trust. It enables the sharing information across a network of participants.

- **Blue Chip** is a large company with a reputation for quality, reliability and the ability to remain profitable in both good times and bad.

- **Bonds** are debt securities. The issuer (borrower) owes a debt to the owners of the bonds. The borrower is typically contracted to pay an annual rate of interest on the bonds and to repay the money borrowed at an agreed date in the future.

- **Bottom up** investors focus their approach on individual companies and assumes that good companies will do well whatever the economic background.

- **Capital** means wealth available for investment.

- **Capital Expenditures** are expenditures to create future benefits.

- **Capital Gains** arise when a security is sold at a profit. It is the difference between the amount paid and the amount realised from a sale.

- **Capital Gains Tax** is payable if the total amount of profit arising from sales of chargeable assets such as shares or property exceeds the government's annual allowance in an individual financial year.

- **Capitalism** is a political system in which trade and industry are controlled by private owners who seek profit, as opposed to the state.

- **Capped Return** refers to the interest rate on a debt security where the interest rate is fixed.

- **Cash** includes bank or building society deposits and other short term financial instruments which share the same attributes as cash.

- **Closed Ended Funds** are collective investment companies such as UK investments trusts that own investments on behalf of their shareholders. When an investor wishes to buy or sell shares in a closed end fund they buy or sell shares in the fund itself. The fund's manager does not therefore need to sell any of the underlying investments to raise the cash to enable investors to realize their holdings.

- **Collective Investment Schemes** are funds which allow investors to invest together in a cost effective and diversified structure.

- **Commission:** a stockbroker's commission is a percentage of the total value of the security being bought or sold that is charged by a broking firm to affect a transaction on behalf of a client. Minimum commission is the lowest amount that a stockbroking firm will accept to transact a trade. If the amount being invested is very small then the minimum commission might represent a significant percentage of the value of the transaction and greatly increase the cost of the investment.

- **Compounding:** the ability of an asset to generate earnings, which are then reinvested in order to generate their own earnings. In other words, compounding refers to generating earnings from previous earnings.

- **Consumer spending or consumer demand,** also known as personal consumption expenditure is a measure of total spending in the economy.

- **Corporation Tax** is a tax payable on a company's profits.

- **Coupon** is a term for the interest payable on debt instruments.

- **Company Pension** is a pension fund set up by a company to provide pensions for its employees.

- **Convertible bonds and preference shares ('Convertibles')** are hybrid securities which combine some of the attributes of bonds and equities. Convertibles typically provide a fixed income return which is higher than the issuing company's share dividend but are convertible into shares at a premium to the current share price at the time of issue.

- **Correlation** refers to the extent to which different types of asset perform in a similar way under the same circumstances.

- **Credit Rating** is a measurement of the risk involved in lending to a company. Ratings are expressed in letter form with the best credits rated at AAA ('Triple A').

- **Credit Risk** is the risk that a borrower may default and fail to pay the interest due on a loan or to repay the loan on the maturity date.

- **Cryptocurrencies** is a digital currency in which transactions are verified and records maintained by a decentralised system using cryptology rather than by a centralised authority.

- **Current Expenditure** is recurring spending on items that are consumed and only last for a limited period of time.

- **Defined Benefits** refer to pension arrangements that relate to a previously agreed level of retirement benefits. The level of pension income is typically a function of the salary that the retiree earned and the number of years that he or she was a member of the pension scheme.

- **Defined Contribution** refers to pension arrangements funded by monetary contributions where the level of post retirement income is dependent on the sum of money that has been contributed to the pension plan and the returns that have been achieved from investing these funds.

- **Derivatives** are types of financial contract whose value is dependent on an underlying asset or group of assets or benchmark such as futures contracts, options or swaps that are often used to hedge investment positions. More exotic derivatives can be based on factors such as weather or carbon emissions.

- **Development Capital** is a form of venture capital at a stage in a company's life when it requires funding to invest and grow.

- **Direct taxation** is the term for taxes such as income tax which are levied directly from taxpayers.

- **Discount** is a word used to describe an asset which is priced below its intrinsic value.

- **Discretionary Expenditure** is defined as costs that are not essential for the operation of a home.

- **Diversification** is a technique that involves the spreading of risk through investment in a range of assets which are not closely correlated.

- **Dividends** are distributions paid by companies to their shareholders.

- **Dividend Cover** is the extent to which a company's dividends are covered by its earnings, or in other words the proportion of its earnings that have been retained as opposed to paid out in dividends.

- **Earnings** is another term for profits.

- **Earnings Per Share (EPS)** is a calculation of a company's profits after tax, divided by the total number of its issued shares.

- **Earnings Yield** is the percentage income yield from a company's shares if they chose to distribute 100% of their earnings to their shareholders.

- **Economics** is a science which studies how individuals, governments and companies allocate scarce resources.

- **Economic Risk** refers to the risk that the outcome for an investment can be affected by the performance of the economies in which a business operates.

- **Endowment Policy** is a life insurance contract designed to pay a lump sum on a specific date or on the death of the policy holder.

- **Equilibrium** is a term describing balance in the economy when supply and demand are in balance.

- **Equity** is another term for shares. After all the costs are paid including interest on loans and taxes, the owners of a company's equity receive the benefit of the assets and earnings.

- **Equity Release** refers to mechanisms that allow home owners to extract a proportion of the value of their properties to supplement income in retirement while continuing to live in their homes.

- **Equity risk** is a level of risk or volatility that is associated with investment in equities.

- **Exchange rate** is the ratio of conversion between currencies.

- **Financial Crash** refers to the global financial crisis in 2008 that is considered by many to have been the most severe since the Great Depression in the 1930's. The build-up of debt that led to the crash threatened the collapse of some of the largest financial institutions.

- **Final Salary Scheme** is another term for a Defined Benefit pension and relates to the link between a beneficiary's leaving salary and the level of pension post retirement.

- **Financial year** is the tax year and in the UK runs from April 6th until April 5th the following calendar year.

- **Fiscal Policy** is the term used for government taxation and spending.

- **Fixed Overheads** are costs that are not directly related to the amount of goods or services produced. Examples include rent or the company's board and management, costs that do not vary with the amount a company produces.

- **Free market economy** is an economy where investment, production, distribution and prices are set by the interchange of supply and demand for goods and services.

- **FTSE 100 Share Index** is an index of the UK's 100 largest companies ranked by the total value of each company's shares.

- **Funds** are sometimes referred to as collective investment schemes. They are structures which enable investors to co-own a much larger and more diverse portfolio of investments than would be possible through direct investments in the fund's underlying assets.

- **Gilt Edged Securities** are fixed interest loans issued by the UK Government, often referred to as 'Gilts'.

- **Government spending** is the money raised by taxes and borrowing that is spent by governments.

- **Gross Salary** means earned income before the deduction of tax and National Insurance Contributions.

- **Gross Yield** is the income from an asset before the deduction of tax.

- **Guarantee** is a term for a contractual responsibility to repay a debt or honour an agreement. A loan guarantee, in finance, is a promise by one party (the guarantor) to assume the debt obligation of a borrower if that borrower defaults. A guarantee can be limited or unlimited, making the guarantor liable for only a portion or all of the debt.

- **Hedge Fund** is a term used to describe a fund that uses advanced investment strategies designed to increase the return, or manage risk, or both.

- **Hyperinflation** is a term for extremely rapid or out of control price inflation.

- **ICB** stands for Industry Classification Benchmark, launched by Dow Jones and FTSE in 2005 to provide industry sector breakdowns of the economy.

- **Illiquid** means difficult or expensive to sell quickly at the asset's full value.

- **An Index** is a method used by investors and fund managers to describe a market and compare the returns of specific investments. It is computed from the prices of selected securities and is typically weighted – meaning that each constituent of an index makes up the same percentage of the index that they represent.

- **Income Tax** is a tax levied on income – either earned through salaries or 'unearned' income from investments.

- **Index Weighting** is the proportion of its index represented by an individual share or an industry sector.

- **Indirect taxes** are taxes such as VAT which are not levied directly from tax payers but are only paid when money is spent on goods and services that attract VAT.

- **Industry piers** is a term for companies in the same businesses against which each company's performance can be fairly measured.

- **Inflation** is the term for an increase in prices.

- **Inheritance Tax** is payable on the value of the sum of the assets of a deceased's estate that exceeds the current level of the tax free allowance.

- **Inland Revenue** was until 2005 the government department responsible for the collection of direct taxes. In April 2005 it was merged with HM Customs and Excise to form HM Revenue and Customs (HMRC).

- **Insolvency** is the inability of a debtor to pay their debts.

- **Interest** is a sum paid by a borrower to a lender in exchange for the loan of funds.

- **IPO** is an Initial Public Offering – a mechanism that sells shares to the general public and enables private companies to be listed on a stock exchange.

- **Irredeemable Bonds** are bonds without a maturity date on which the lenders are repaid.

- **Keynesian economics** is the view that in the short term is strongly influenced by demand in the economy which can best be managed by fiscal policy – government taxation and spending.

- **Liabilities** are obligations to pay. In an accounting context a liability is an obligation from a past transaction or event. In the context of investment the term is applied to the requirement to match investments to future liabilities such as school fees or living expenses post retirement.

- **Liquidity** refers to cash and other assets that are easy and cheap to sell and return to cash.

- **Listed securities** are investments that are tradable on a recognized exchange. Exchanges have their own listing requirements designed to ensure that investments listed and traded meet certain quality requirements – and to protect the reputation of the exchange.

- **Market Risk** refers to the extent that the returns from an investment are influenced by factors that affect the overall performance of financial markets.

- **Market Timing** is a term which describes the timing of the purchase or sales of investments.

- **Maturity Date** is the date when a borrower is contractually bound to repay a loan.

- **Monetarists** believe that economic output and inflation can best be managed by controlling money supply and interest rates.

- **Monetary Asset** is an asset such as cash or a debt where the value is fixed.

- **Money Purchase** is another term for a Defined Contribution pension arrangement.

- **Money supply** is the total quantity of monetary assets available in an economy.

- **Mortgage** is a term used to describe a mortgage loan that is secured on a specific asset such as a property.

- **Net Asset Value (NAV)** is the value of an asset after subtracting all liabilities including loans and other creditors. When used in the context of an investment trust the NAV is the value attributable to each individual share.

- **Net yield** is the income yield after paying tax.

- **Non-Discretionary Expenditure** is spending which is essential for the operation of a home.

- **Normal Distribution** – Data can be 'distributed' (spread out) in different ways.

It can be spread out more on the left.

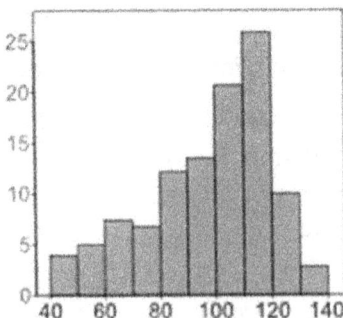

or more on the right

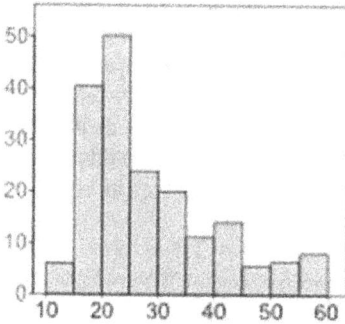

Or it can be all jumbled up

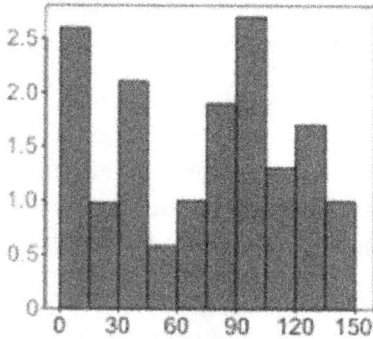

But there are many cases where the data tends to be around a central value with no bias left or right, and it gets close to a 'Normal Distribution' like this:

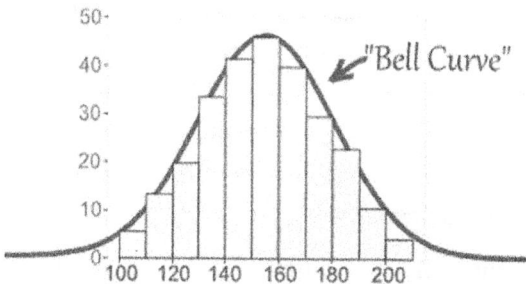

The 'Bell Curve' is a Normal Distribution.

193

- **Old Age:** Three old men are talking about their aches, pains and bodily functions. One seventy-year-old man says: 'I have this problem. I wake up every morning at seven and it takes me twenty minutes to pee.'

  An eighty-year-old man says: 'My case is worse. I get up at eight and I sit there and grunt and groan for half an hour before I finally have a bowel movement.'

  The ninety-year-old man says: At seven I pee like a horse, at eight I crap like a cow.'

  'So what's your problem?' asked the others.

  'I don't wake up until nine.'

- **On demand** is a term used to describe overdraft loans that must immediately be repaid on the demand of the lender.

- **Open Ended Funds** are collective investment schemes that receive funds from new investors, which the managers then invest. Investors who wish to sell have their redemptions met by either the sale of assets within the fund or through the funds subscribed by new investors.

- **Overhead costs** is a term for an ongoing expense which is not directly related to the amount of business being contracted such as rent and rates.

- **Paper** loss is the assumed loss on an investment before the investment is sold and the loss becomes an actual realised loss.

- **Par value** is the maturity value of a bond.

- **Pension Fund** is a tax privileged funding arrangement – either with Defined Benefits or via Defined Contributions – set up to provide retirement benefits for one or more beneficiaries.

- **Personal Pensions** are pension plans in tax privileged investment vehicles set up to provide pension benefits to individuals.

- **Political Risk** is the risk that investment returns can be affected by political instability or when political decisions adversely affect investment returns.

- **Ponzi scheme** means an investment fraud that pays existing investors with funds raised from new investors.

- **Preference Share** is a form of equity that generates a fixed rate of return. They have close similarities with bonds but returns tend to be higher because although interest must be paid in full before dividends can be paid to ordinary shareholders, preference shareholders rank behind the creditors for payment and cannot force the sale of assets to gain interest or secure repayment. There can be certain tax and structural advantages for both issuers and investors because preference shares are a form of equity capital and are not debt instruments.

- **Price Earnings Ratio** is a measure of share valuation calculated by dividing a company's share price by the net earnings after interest and tax to arrive at the profit attributable to each share. The ratio is expressed a share price's multiple of earnings.

- **Private Equity** is the generic term for investment in the equity and debt of companies that are not publicly traded on a stock exchange.

- **Productivity** means the efficiency of production.

- **Profit** means sales revenue minus costs.

- **Progressive taxation** is any tax in which the rate of tax increases as the amount subject to the tax increases.

- **Purchasing Power Parity** is the theory that relative exchange rates between currencies should move reflect parity in the amounts that both currencies can buy.

- **Quoted Shares** are shares quoted on a stock exchange.

- **Rating Agencies** are companies that specialize in the analysis of borrowers' ability to pay interest and repay their loans.

- **Real Assets** are assets that have a real tangible value such as gold and property. Although traditional descriptions have often excluded equities from the definition, when used in the context of the quest for 'real' returns adjusted for the effects of inflation, equities are included within the definition of real assets.

- **Real Return** is the investment return over and above inflation. An investment which merely keeps pace with inflation provides no real return and an investment that does not even match inflation provides a negative real return.

- **Redemption** is a term for the repayment of a loan or the sale of a unit or share in an open ended collective investment fund.

- **Run on a bank** occurs when a large number of customers lose confidence and withdraw their money from a bank.

- **Shares** is another word for 'Equities' described above.

- **Shorting** is a practice where investors sell shares that they do not own in order to benefit from a fall in the share price. The transaction involves the borrowing of shares in exchange for a small fee that allows the borrower to sell and 'go short'. To undo the trade the investor buys the shares back and takes a profit if the price has fallen or loss if it has risen.

- **Standard Deviation** is a measurement of historic volatility. If the historic spread of outcomes is normal than the Standard Deviation offers an indication of the expected range of future outcomes. The higher the Standard Deviation, the wider the expected range of outcomes.

- **State Pension** is a pension provided by the government. It is a contributions based pension related to the beneficiaries' National Insurance Contribution history.

- **Stealth Tax** is a tax which goes unnoticed or is not recognized as a tax because does not hit the taxpayers either obviously or immediately.

- **Sterling** is the traditional name for the UK's currency, the Pound Sterling.

- **Terms of trade** is the relative price of a country's exports in terms of imports.

- **Top down** investing focuses on the bigger picture rather than the underlying detail, emphasizing the significance of economic and market cycles.

- **Unearned income** is income derived from investments and other sources unrelated to employment.

- **Variable costs** are costs which are directly related to the amount of activity that rise or fall accordingly.

- **Velocity of circulation** is a term used by economists describing the rate at which money in circulation within an economy is used for purchasing goods and services and circulates within the economy.

- **Venture Capital** is a traditional generic term for Private Equity. Current usage tends to imply high risk investments in start-up ventures.

- **Yield** is the annual income return from a security – interest from cash and bonds or dividends from shares – expressed as a percentage that the income represents as a proportion of the value of the security.

- **Yield Gap** is the additional yield that an investor might receive from an investment in Gilts when compared to an investment in the equities. A Reverse Yield Gap is the term for the additional yield that investors have for periods received from an investment in the equity indices compared to an investment in Gilts.

- **Zero** dividend preference shares provide income from capital appreciation and are therefore taxed as capital gain and not income.

Notes

www.ingramcontent.com/pod-product-compliance
Lightning Source LLC
Chambersburg PA
CBHW020201200326
41521CB00005BA/207

* 9 7 8 1 8 0 3 8 1 9 5 4 9 *